The 5 States of Success

The 5 States of Success

Create *meaningful* success
in your career, business & life

Brendan Foley

MERCIER PRESS
IRISH PUBLISHER – IRISH STORY

MERCIER PRESS

Cork

www.mercierpress.ie

ISBN: 978 1 85635 804 0

10 9 8 7 6 5 4 3 2 1

A CIP record for this title is available from the British Library

Printed and bound in the EU.

Contents

For Sarah, Patrick and Finn – All my love

Introduction

Hello and thanks for picking up this book. You might be thinking about buying it – if so, buy it, it will change the way you think for the better! If you have already bought this book then congratulations, you have by your intention and willingness to develop yourself taken a step closer to *meaningful* success.

In this book, I will challenge your notions of success and help you to clarify what *meaningful* success is to you. If you are looking for a book that will give you practical tools and an understanding of the context of when and where to use them, you have come to the right place.

I would like to set my stall out early and tell you exactly what you will get from this book. Over the past twenty years, ever since I first became involved in high-level international sport, I have searched to find the key ingredients that make up success. Over that period there were many times when I was convinced I had found the formula, only to discover another element being revealed. I feel that I have now identified those ingredients, but I will let you be the judge of that.

My approach to working with businesses and people to create success is based on the insights gained from deep personal experience and the wonderful opportunity I have had to connect to thousands of people through my work as a life and business coach, trainer, motivational speaker and facilitator. My journey has brought me into contact with what would be considered some of the most successful people in many walks of life, from sport, to medicine, to spirituality, to business. The journey has helped me to identify five key 'states' of being that will allow you to create *meaningful* success in your career, business and life. They are:

The State of INSIGHT – creates *CLARITY* to allow logical and creative thinking to unite.

The State of CONNECTION – creates *EMPATHY* to build relationships with others.

The State of CERTAINTY – creates *CONVICTION* to proceed, based on intuitive wisdom.

The State of VITALITY – creates *ACTION* to create real and *meaningful* success.

The State of SPIRIT – creates *PURPOSE* that builds uniqueness and leadership.

It is in these five states that some of the most remarkable success stories take place. They are found in every person, team and business, but are demonstrated to varying degrees.

We will explore each of these states and, using stories, tools, techniques and insights, you will learn how to harness and utilise these innate powers. Each success state produces or brings forth an ability that will result in the team, company or individual displaying *clarity, empathy, certainty, vitality* and *purpose*: a potent cocktail of traits guaranteed to create success.

THE 5 STATES OF SUCCESS

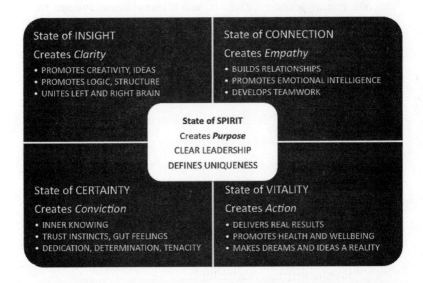

State of INSIGHT

Creates *Clarity*

- PROMOTES CREATIVITY, IDEAS
- PROMOTES LOGIC, STRUCTURE
- UNITES LEFT AND RIGHT BRAIN

State of CONNECTION

Creates *Empathy*

- BUILDS RELATIONSHIPS
- PROMOTES EMOTIONAL INTELLIGENCE
- DEVELOPS TEAMWORK

State of SPIRIT

Creates ***Purpose***

CLEAR LEADERSHIP

DEFINES UNIQUENESS

State of CERTAINTY

Creates *Conviction*

- INNER KNOWING
- TRUST INSTINCTS, GUT FEELINGS
- DEDICATION, DETERMINATION, TENACITY

State of VITALITY

Creates *Action*

- DELIVERS REAL RESULTS
- PROMOTES HEALTH AND WELLBEING
- MAKES DREAMS AND IDEAS A REALITY

To make them easy to recall and to understand the nature of the **5 States of Success**, each state corresponds with a part of the body. The State of Insight is connected with the head, the place where our ideas are born and intellectual capacities for clarity lie. The State of Connection is like the heart, the symbol of relationships, which are built on empathy. The State of Certainty is like our gut, the place we get our feelings of intuition from and our drive and conviction. The State of Vitality connects with our health and the whole physical body, which provides us with the ability to take action. Finally the State of Spirit, which is represented by the intangible and animating force of life inside us all, provides us with our sense of purpose.

We can also connect each of the **5 States of Success** to one of the ancient elements. The State of Insight is like the element of air: our thoughts move and change like the wind. The State of Connection is like water: emotions flowing and ebbing. The State of Certainty is like earth: our gut instincts that are sure, strong and reliable. The State of Vitality is like fire: bringing action, excitement and change. The State of Spirit is like ether: intangible and unseen but crucial in providing a business or life purpose.

STATE	ABILITY	CAPACITY	ELEMENT	PHYSIOLOGY
Insight	Clarity	Thinking	Air	Head
Connection	Empathy	Emotion	Water	Heart
Certainty	Conviction	Intuition	Earth	Gut
Vitality	Action	Movement	Fire	Body
Spirit	Purpose	Animation	Ether	Life force

Each state produces an ability or trait that is highly desirable in the quest for *meaningful* success. What business or person would not want to have the attributes of *clarity*, *empathy*, *conviction*, *action* and *purpose*? Engaging with the **5 States of Success** brings out these wonderful abilities.

When you start to use and combine the **5 States of Success** – Insight, Connection, Certainty, Vitality and Spirit – on a daily basis, you will create a personal, team or business culture that will accomplish your ultimate goal, *meaningful* success, which brings happiness, health and wealth!

READING GUIDE

This book is divided not into chapters (as that implies that there is a sequence in which this book must be read), but rather into parts. Each part on its own will help you to master the title concept of that section and so can be read and practised in its own right. That said, reading the parts consecutively will allow you to get a very clear picture of the landscape of *meaningful* success and help you to clearly identify where you can make changes in your life, team or business to create the success that you desire. Think of this book as a tool kit or companion that you can access to gain inspiration or techniques to better cope with or master the situation that you currently find yourself, your team or your business in.

Opinion will be divided on many of the examples of people and companies used in this book and on whether they can really be considered great or inspirational. In referring to them I will be referring to qualities that they may possess that can lead to *meaningful* success. This does not mean that they are perfect: what is important is to see and understand how they exemplify the 'State' being discussed.

Most of all try to enjoy this read, because *meaningful* success does not mean adhering to every word or having to memorise every technique. The beauty of this book is that *you* will have already experienced the **5 States of Success** in your life. What I will do is show you how to create these states on a consistent basis. All you have to do is to bring them into your consciousness so that profound success flows to you, your team, business or organisation.

OK. Let the journey begin!

What Does Success Mean to You?

Meaningful success is the type of success that creates happiness, health and wealth.

Brendan Foley

So what does success mean to you? This question can lead you to the truth of what you do and how you do it. For most of us the answer is informed by other people's success and our hunger to have what they have (or at least what we perceive they have!). It may also be informed by our parents, schooling, social conditioning and a host of other environmental and cultural factors that create the state of being which we define as 'successful'.

Through the coaching, training and motivation work I have done, and in my own personal and business experience, I have discovered that success is a very relative state that is in constant flux. For example, today my goal may be to complete this section and if I do, I will deem this day a success. Yet some years ago after a car crash, success was getting back to doing the simplest things in life, things that I took for granted. I am sure you have similar stories. What they teach us is: *success is relative to your needs on any given day.*

One of the most common definitions of success I come across in the personal setting concerns what is termed financial freedom, or the ability to do whatever you want because you don't have to earn a living from it. In my view, the notion of financial freedom is a complete fallacy. One reason is that there is no such thing as ultimate financial freedom. It is a fantasy that we have been sold by pedlars of investment funds and get rich quick schemes. We are told to accumulate resources and wealth to achieve this so-called state of freedom. What actually happens is that we acquire a lovely set of 'golden handcuffs'! I mean that all our possessions actually become traps that deprive us of the very freedom we were meant to be achieving by having them. Every item you collect – property, cars and so on – comes with responsibilities and, of course, running costs. We have to stretch further to pay for these and therefore need to accumulate more. We also get the lovely gift of the fear associated with trying to hang on to these possessions. After a few years of this type of living we become so entrenched in the cycle of accumulation, we completely lose sight of why we ever wanted or needed these things.

This cycle of accumulation is fully supported by the culture and economy that we live in, so that we arrive at a situation where the behaviour of accumulation becomes classed as normal. By asking yourself what success means to you, you can break this cycle by refocusing on what it is YOU want in your life rather than sleepwalking in an infinite loop of ceaseless accumulation. Some of the most free and happy people I have met are those who consider themselves abundant at all times and are without the need for material satisfaction. In case you think these people are hermits living in nature and outside modern society, many of them are considered highly successful business people; they have plenty, but they do not have an attachment to the material items in their lives and do not allow themselves to be identified or given status by their assets. Ask yourself a question: do you associate feelings of well-being with the assets and possessions you are attached to? If so, you are their prisoner and as such are at their whim, because if they are removed from you, you will feel a lesser person.

An ancient Indian legend expresses the attachment we have to our possessions beautifully:

There was a handsome and wealthy Raj who had many farms, a beautiful family with many fine children, a loving wife, many palaces and gardens, wonderful friends, beautiful jewels and treasures and countless works of art. Not only was he rich but he was also wise. He realised that in all he had if he possessed it too tightly it would destroy him with worry and anxiety over protecting this great fortune. So every night when he went to bed he imagined his farms had collapsed under drought, his family and children had abandoned him, his many fine palaces and gardens were destroyed in an earthquake, his friends all died of fever, his jewel and art collection were stolen. So as he went to sleep, he slept as a man with nothing to lose and his sleep was sound.

When he would awake in the morning to see his love lying beside him he would be filled with great joy and wonder; when he embraced his children he did so like a man returned from the dead; when he saw his artwork and treasure he was filled with glee and admiration of their workmanship; when he met his friends he greeted them with the gusto of meeting long lost companions; and when he surveyed all that he owned he was filled with huge gratitude and happiness.

I love this story as it captures the thoughtless attachment that we have to our possessions and shows us how we can become dim and unaware of the great treasures all around us. Now I would not go as far as to recommend visualising losing everything, but the point is well made in the story.

If you are thinking about business or your career in terms of success, this can become another trap, if you let it. I meet many people who do great work but who complain that the only reason they work so hard is to provide for their family and for their family's happiness. The irony here is that if your family had a choice they would not want more possessions, they would want you and your time. As you can see there is a pattern emerging here with two major themes: lack of awareness of what you really value and an attachment to something that creates fear. To counteract these very powerful forces we really need to understand what success means to each of us.

THE GARDEN OF LIFE

To help you do this it is very worthwhile to look at your life as being a garden. Each area of your life will be represented in your plot. For example your family may be the fruit bushes and trees, your health may be hedges and borders, your career or business the lawns, your education and hobbies the shed, your spirituality the pond and fountain, and finally your voluntary contribution the rose bushes and shrubs. As in life, you will tend more carefully the areas that you enjoy most or feel are most important. Maybe you are passionate about your lawns (career) and cultivate them with care and attention. If this is the case then you will have immaculate lawns of stunning green (or a very successful career). But what is happening to the rest of your garden? Are the fruit bushes and trees (your family) becoming overgrown and stifled by your lack of attention? Is the garden shed getting dusty and cobweb covered (in other words are your education and learning growing old and stale)? While you are tending your lawns with such care what is happening to the borders and hedges (your health)? Are they top heavy and in risk of collapse?

The analogy of the garden of life helps us to recognise all the areas that make up a fulfilling and happy existence and that they all require attention and care. This is never more important than when we consider what success means to us. Success in one area of your life only is just an illusion of success, as what is in fact often happening is an imbalance. We are creatures of balance and whether it is a business, a team or a person, balanced success across a range of areas is true success.

Exercise

- Look at the headings below and, using a scale from 1 to 10 where 1 is very poor and 10 is excellent, score the areas of your life in terms of how much attention you give to each.

An overview of where you are investing the time in your life	
Health/Fitness	
Sport/Hobbies	
Wealth/Finance	
Career/Business	
Family/Relationships	

Friends/Social	
Contribution/Voluntary work	
Spirituality/Purpose	
Education/Learning	

How did you score? You may be realising that you have over-invested your energy and time in some areas of your life to the detriment of others. Your score will also be very dependent on your stage of life and the current cycle of activity you are engaged in.

Quite recently this issue arose for one of my clients who wanted to undertake a master's degree in business. He has a full-time job that was prepared to support him with a half day off every Friday, but he would be required to study every evening during the week and attend classes at the weekend. He has four children and a wife. We quickly realised that if he was to take on the master's study then he would score very highly on the Education and Learning scale, but that this would negatively impact on the time he would have available for Family/Relationships, his Sport/Hobbies and his Friends/Social, and by not having those outlets his Health/Fitness would also suffer. Having received this insight he relooked at his need for learning and decided to do a module-based master's degree over five years rather than two years. By doing this he could achieve a healthy balance in his life and ultimately create more happiness. By recognising the consequences of his decision early, he could tend to the 'garden of life' in a way that would reward him and not create family problems which might lead to him abandoning his studies.

> **Exercise**
> - Think about what you want to achieve and how it will affect your garden of life.
> - Do you need to adjust your goals?

WHAT MAKES YOUR HEART SOAR?

This question provides the answer to what creates success and happiness in your life. It is both a challenging and a freeing question as it asks us if we are ready to be happy doing what we love. Or will we keep pedalling along on the hamster wheel of life dreaming about what we could do rather than ever truly engaging with this question?

To ask this question and to be prepared to follow the outcome, or answer, requires bravery. Most people you will meet in your life will 'toe the line' and do what others think are the right things for them to do. In my opinion very few people are brave enough to step outside the conventional or traditional view of life to explore living their dream. This is why so few people ultimately reach the high pinnacles of human achievement and happiness. I believe those who surrender to what makes their heart soar create massive happiness and by default produce what others would consider mighty achievements.

What would you be doing now if there were no barriers, no rules and all your expenses would be paid for one year? Many people will flippantly make statements such as 'living on a desert island', 'not working', 'driving a Ferrari'. However, when pressed you start to see the real magic begin to happen. As people share what really gives them a great sense of well-being their eyes light up, their pulse quickens, they relax and their gaze goes into the middle distance as they describe in brilliant, emotive and evocative terms what truly inspires or motivates them. Their true calling. Then, as suddenly as the dream started, they are hauled back into the reality of their lives and become dismissive about achieving their dream, usually because 'that won't pay the bills' or other such excuses.

In my experience, the magic actually ensures a person will be a huge success in their chosen field or calling. This is where we start to see that what people really want is vocations, not jobs. I define a vocation as something you would do because you love it so much, even if you were never paid for it! When you connect to what makes your heart fly high your passion becomes infectious; this makes you highly attractive and valuable to others and by default, and not design, you will be able to earn your living from your calling.

For example, a friend of mine is an incredible artist, but works in sales. He is good at both painting and sales, but what truly makes him happy is his artwork. He has had several very successful exhibitions but refuses the call of his creativity as he hangs onto the sales job because it gives him security and stability. Is this also you? Conversely I know bankers who have become trainers, software engineers who have become sports therapists, human resource managers who have become alternative medicine practitioners, advertising executives who have become chefs, and nearly all are happy and successful, or on their way to getting there.

You may ask, 'But how do I pay my bills while I make a transition or explore myself?' In my experience, I have found that people are very resourceful when they take the leap of faith to pursue a new direction. If the direction is right for you, you will be filled with energy and excitement that allows you to find sources of finance. Some people start new businesses by night or at the weekend while holding down a job. Many people find that once they make a commitment to change, savings, an unexpected windfall, a surprise investor or backer, or the opportunity to be paid for what you wish to do serendipitously appears. I believe many of these new sources of revenue can be attracted at a subconscious level where we are able to identify opportunities that we were previously blind to.

REALISATIONS

I speak from first-hand experience. I have always loved communications, whether it is TV, advertising or any type of graphic format. My path took me through an honours degree in marketing to a professional post in advertising and from there into a series of advertising and marketing roles. I was very good at what I did and rapidly rose to the top of the profession. What I discovered in my work was that I was always given people to work with who were considered difficult clients. I saw this as a challenge, not about the client being tough, but more about my ability to find the right words and manner in which to connect with those clients. During this time I won industry awards and surprised myself at what I could achieve, but something was gnawing at me. Something I did not fully understand yet.

In 2005, three weeks before my wedding, my father had a terrible accident and a few weeks after the wedding he passed away. This blew my world apart. While tragic, however, it also held a positive aspect. It made me step back from my life and get some perspective on myself. I discovered that in the busyness of being busy I had been a brilliant goal achiever, as when I thought about something I wanted, I would go after it and usually get it. I also discovered, though, that I was not a good goal maker. I had never taken the time to ask what I really wanted and was caught up in the rat race of modern life. I believe if I was still in advertising today I would have burned out with the speed I was moving at. I realised after my father's passing that life is too valuable not to spend it the way you really want and in a way that can make you and others happy. This was the gnawing feeling that I had had, a feeling that I could be something different, could be helping others while still achieving personally. While I did not have the words to express it, what I had stumbled upon was the idea of living a life defined by *meaningful* success.

On a three-day seminar by Tony Robbins, an American motivational speaker, that my employers had arranged for the team in the office, I had my big moment. I realised that my love of sailing was not so much about winning as about what makes teams and people winners. I realised my career had brought out a skill in me to help people understand themselves and to communicate their message. I realised that a life well lived is a life that feels purposeful and in some way can serve a greater good. So I decided to get into the area of helping people to achieve their potential and established my training and coaching company, Seachange Training (www.seachangetraining.com).

Paralleling this new beginning for me in coaching and training, I also had great success in my chosen sport and passion, yacht racing. Along with my team, we won first the UK National Championships with all first places and then the French National Championships, again with all first places, and we finished second in the Offshore Sailing

World Championships (Commodores' Cup 2006). Both the business and sporting success came from realising that what really lights my fire and makes my heart soar like an eagle is creating personal success, being of service to others, motivating others and helping them see their own brilliance.

I started my business in an economic depression, giving up a solid job with great prospects (as others saw it). A business consultant or financial advisor would have told me not to do this, as the training and coaching business was beginning to feel the effects of the recession. But I had something that their spreadsheets and predictions could not calculate – passion and belief. These were ignited and flowed infinitely because I took the bold step to follow my dream. It was a very frightening step to take, to jump out on my own and pursue a career that did not have a career path or best practice route. I am happy to say that today I am fulfilling my purpose and am as passionate now, if not more so, as I was the day I started my business. I am also happy to say my business is very successful. I believe that part of my continuing success is because I regularly ask myself, 'What makes my heart soar?' When I get a good feeling, I go with it and so does the business. When I find we are doing business that does not make our hearts soar, we move on to what does. As a friend of mine beautifully puts it, 'follow your bliss' – a line from the author Joseph Campbell. By living and breathing what we really love, we create *meaningful* success. I hope that you might take from my story the belief to do what you have always wanted to do or change what your company does to reflect your passions and desires.

BUT I DON'T KNOW WHAT I REALLY WANT TO DO

I have to admit that most people when really pressed find it hard to identify the 'job' or 'career' that they are most attracted to or that would fulfil their sense of life purpose. Most people make the mistake of believing that a life purpose or most fulfilling way to make a living are the same as a job or career. As long as people interpret the question in this way then they will struggle to find what they are looking for. If we separate out what we know as jobs or careers and focus instead on the feeling state or the patterns that exist behind what we love in our lives, then we can identify or create roles and careers that will satisfy these desires.

Arun's story helps to illustrate this point. Arun (not his real name), when faced with the question of how to progress in his career, was struggling. He held a top international post in a very large software company. He had graduated top of his class from his university in India and been headhunted by a large American software firm. He rose rapidly through the ranks of this organisation and such was his skill he was always on the move with new companies and being given new assignments in different countries. When I met him through a coaching assignment, he was at a crossroads in his life. His mother had recently passed away and he was starting to question and evaluate where he wanted to go with his career. He had three main avenues open to him: promotion within his existing company, moving to a competitor or setting up his own company. Arun had never really chosen a path. He had fallen into opportunity after opportunity.

When I asked him, 'Do you love what you do?', he looked like a rabbit caught in the headlights and was very wary of the question, retorting: 'Why is that important? Do you have to love what you do?'

I replied, 'No, you don't *have* to do anything but would you *like* to do what you love?'

'Yes,' he replied.

We went on to discover that he did not love software or IT and he started to get very frustrated with himself because he could not immediately identify what it was he did love.

Realising this I changed tack. 'What do you love outside of work?'

'I love music, I have learned to play three instruments … I love understanding new cultures … I love cooking and new recipes … I love playing sports …'

'Great.' We were now getting into what I describe as golden territory, the place where we all start to shine as we speak about those things we love with passion.

Arun explained that he had this great love of new things, people and challenges. But he started to become negative again, saying, 'I can't make a living out of any of those things I love …'

Over the course of the next hour we looked for the common factor or thread that linked all the disparate things he loved together. What was the big feature behind all the things he loved? What was the desire that drove his passion? In a moment of total clarity (State of Insight), he understood it.

'I know, I love learning!' he exclaimed.

Arun's problem was not that he did not know what he wanted to do in life, he had just never questioned what it was that he truly loved. The sport, the music, the cooking were all symptoms of the underlying desire – a love of learning. Armed with this knowledge he suddenly saw that he did not have to stay in IT or software, or, alternatively, he could stay in that field as long as he had a position that allowed him to learn. We worked out that it would help if he was surrounded by people who also loved learning, which meant that the most suitable of the career options for him would need to demonstrate these qualities.

He became excited as he started to see that he could use his knowledge of the Internet and business as a venture capitalist to help to fund new and emerging technologies, an area that would require constant learning. He started to see that he could look for roles within his current company that would involve plenty of innovation. The answers were always there for Arun and his passion was the key to unlocking them.

> **Exercise**
> • Can you identify the desires that are behind what you really love? What are they?

FEELING WHAT YOU LOVE

Another way to find what drives you, and to identify what you should be investing your life in, can come from accessing the feeling states of your life. I mentioned earlier the golden territory. This is a key indicator to me as to when people are being true to themselves about what they love. There is an undeniable shift in people's posture and body language when they start to discuss what it is that they truly love. They light up, become more vibrant and energised and you can almost see their heart start to lift with passion.

Take Elizabeth (not her real name), a very talented and successful engineer who I worked with. She came to me because her business was struggling and she was expecting to have a conversation based on how she could sell in a more effective manner or how she could improve her marketing to make her business more successful. As she discussed her business and her problems in attracting new business, I sensed something

31

was not quite right. When I pushed Elizabeth to talk about what she loved about engineering she rolled out some well-rehearsed 'positive talk' or spin that she obviously told herself and her friends and family about how much she enjoyed her business. I was left completely unmoved by what she told me and the glazed, heavy look in her eyes as she spoke told another truth. This was not a woman living her passion. Probing further still I asked Elizabeth why she had set up her business – it was an escape from a large international utility company where she felt unappreciated and unmotivated. At first she had great success with this move but as the years passed her energy and passion had waned.

I challenged Elizabeth with a simple statement: 'Are you a product of the company you created or is the company a product of you?'

Elizabeth seemed confused by my question. I rephrased: 'The feelings that helped you to create this company were passion and enthusiasm, but you seem to now be a prisoner of your company and the feelings that are being created in you are apathy and worry.'

It was like she had been hit by a freight train. Elizabeth realised that the very vehicle she had created to give herself freedom was now trapping her. The warders of her captivity were the expectations of others that she would create great success, the fear of admitting that maybe she did not love what she had put herself out there as and the shame in admitting defeat.

I asked Elizabeth to then tell me where in her life she found feelings of being energised and uplifted. She could immediately tell me: 'in my music'. She told me she was a classically trained musician and that with all the stress she had been feeling this outlet was like breaths of new life to a drowning woman. As she spoke, her slumped and tired posture seemed to rise up and brightness and lightness spread across her face. Her eyes sparkled as she recalled recent times playing the cello. She spoke with passion about the community of musicians she interacted with and the wonderful fulfilment she felt while playing.

I asked Elizabeth to look behind the positive feelings and to identify what it was about playing classical music that had such a positive effect on her emotional state. After much exploration, three major themes emerged: creativity, community and technical precision. I then asked her if she found any of these themes in her business. She could see where the precision on the practical side of her business came through, but there was no creativity and no community. Suddenly she knew that she did not need a new sales and marketing strategy, but instead needed to bring creativity and community into her business. She left uplifted and determined to carry the feeling states created by her music into her business. In doing so she would no longer be a product of her business; instead, her business would be a product of her positive feeling state. She introduced creativity by organising training for her team on how to think imaginatively and problem solve, and brought a spirit of community to life by creating social outlets and opportunities for people in the business to get to know each other and collaborate on exciting research projects.

Exercise

Personal

- What are the feeling states behind the things you love doing most, and are they reflected in your work?

Business/team

- If you work in a business or team, ask the same question of the collective group – do we do what we love?

THE 'YOU'RE GREAT AT THAT' TRAP

What is interesting to consider when reflecting on the two previous stories is that we often find ourselves going from day to day without any real awareness of how we are feeling, in particular about our careers. What I also commonly encounter is people who are very successful but not happy and this is often because they have outgrown their situation, in terms of learning, passion and responsibility. Many of us witnessed our parents having just one career or a 'job for life'.

We are also continually shown in the media archetypes of success, who tend to be people in the sporting, business or social arenas who have done just one thing or are known for just one thing. Think of Seamus Heaney in poetry and literature, Tony Robbins in self-development, Bill Cullen in business and Michael Schumacher in Formula 1 racing. There is nothing wrong with this, but it often encourages the collective mindset to assume that to be successful we need to identify one life path or career choice, and to stick at it until we are successful.

Compounding the limitations of the fact that many people believe the perfect career has to be for life, is the way in which we come to select our chosen career or profession. When we were young, somebody may have commented on and maybe even celebrated a talent or ability that we had. Here we enter the 'You're great at that' trap. As we grew we developed strategies to get attention from adults. Picture if you will the family with four children. One kid starts to have sporting success and the parents encourage this as a positive trait and use of energy. Another child demonstrates an early aptitude with numbers and so this trait is encouraged. The other two children are seen as funny and artistic respectively. Chances are that these early empowerments actually set up learning patterns for the rest of the children's lives. We might then encounter the family thirty years on and find we have an accountant, a designer, a sports person and someone working in communications. Yet none may actually be doing something they truly love. Perhaps the accountant has the ability to be a golfing masters champion but will never let himself try. Perhaps the designer has a love of numbers but because she went to art college and has many years' experience as a designer, she feels she cannot follow her passion for maths. Are you one of these children?

Not everyone is in the wrong role or career, but there are very many people in businesses who, if they could play to their strengths and passions, their levels of fulfilment and happiness would increase and then an exponential effect would be had on the success of the business or team they work with. Almost every modern psychometric tool (describing character or working traits), from Belbin, Myers Briggs, McQuaig to CPQ, advocates that if people are involved in roles where they can use their best character and working traits to good effect, then they are happier and the business is more successful. My anecdotal assessment is that up to 60% of people in most companies are doing the wrong jobs. This means in essence that 40% of employees have to carry the other 60%. Even if you can tip the scales slightly in favour of people in the right roles, the results are stunning.

This is important: if a part of your psyche holds a belief system that says 'your passion in life equals only one career', then dump this! Many of the people who create *meaningful* success do so because they do not allow themselves to become stuck in a rut. Even if it means a massive change in what they are doing, the bravest will be prepared to follow what they love and have passion for. Steve Jobs, the founder of Apple Computing, is a great example of this. He had always wanted to go to college, but when he did he did not take the courses he was supposed to; instead he went to calligraphy classes. At the time, this would have seemed mad, but many years later when he founded Apple he incorporated beautiful fonts into his machines – a direct influence from his days in Berkeley.[1] Or look at former US Vice President Al Gore, who moved from White House politician to anti-climate change campaigner and evangelist. Caroline Casey, the Irish social entrepreneur, formerly a management consultant with Accenture, now heads up KANCHI, an organisation that brings together disability and business, and is founder of the O2 Ability Awards. Reinvention of your career allows your real and true passions to have a form of expression and then you can create *meaningful* success.

All my work has led me to believe that the success you wish to achieve can happen as long as you are conscious in your decision to be in the **5 States of Success**: insight, connection, certainty, vitality and spirit. These performance states allow you to consistently produce clarity, empathy,

---

1   Search 'Steve Jobs Stanford speech' on YouTube to see an inspirational clip.

conviction, action and purpose that delivers *meaningful* success. When your heart flies high and you operate from a positive feeling state, I believe that you unlock the potential for these states to exist and will create personal success, team success and business success. By looking at your career in a different light, you can carve out a niche in the world that will allow you to create *meaningful* success.

Exercise

Personal

- Ask yourself now – what makes your heart fly high?

  It can be very helpful to write a list or keep a notebook close and ask yourself that question for seven days. You will be amazed at what comes up!

Business/team

- Find out – what makes others in your team or business buzz?

  If you are part of a management team – ask your colleagues and staff what success means to them.

Part 1 –
The State of Insight

The State of INSIGHT – creates *CLARITY*
- Promotes creativity and ideas
- Promotes logic and structure
- Unites left and right brain
- Memory trigger: your head, element of air

The State of Insight's gift of clarity of thought allows us to gain a unique grasp of complex matters. When we are in a State of Insight we utilise both the left and right hemispheres of our brains, connecting logic and creativity. Complex matters become simple and straightforward when we are in a State of Insight. As Stephen Covey says in his book *The 7 Habits of Highly Effective People*, 'what I wouldn't give for the simplicity on the far side of complexity!'

We all are aware that when our thoughts are cluttered and confused we lack the ability to communicate clearly or to identify the right choices. By getting ourselves into the State of Insight, we become a source of illumination to those around us and we cut through the fog of confusion. When we are insightful we allow the ability to process information, which each of us possesses, to unfold.

THE AGE OF INTELLIGENCE?

If you are reading this book you will already be very proficient at absorbing information and out of it selecting the key data that will allow you to move closer to your intended goal. As Tony Buzan, the founder of MindMaps and one of the world's most influential thinkers, says, 'we are now living in the age of intelligence'.[2] Our ability to process vast quantities of information and from it elicit the most important data has never been more important. We have moved from the Industrial Revolution, to the technological age, to the information age and now to the age of intelligence (I believe we may even be

---

2   Tony Buzan, in the National Concert Hall, Dublin, Ireland, 18 October 2010.

beyond this age already and are in the age of empathy; more on this in Part 2: The State of Connection). If you google the word 'information' you get access to 3,100,000,000 records or 3.1 billion pieces of information in 0.29 seconds. Your access to information is staggering. Think about this for a moment. What amount of data did your parents have access to? What amount of data did your grandparents have access to? They had to do research by writing away or travelling great distances to access books, libraries and people with knowledge. You start to realise that there has never been a time when so many people have had so much instant access to so much information. It is clear to see that access to information is not the challenge of this age, rather our challenge is twofold: where to access information that is accurate and how to create useful insights from it.

THE HEAD, AIR AND INSIGHT

As an *aide-mémoire*, or memory trigger, it is useful to connect the State of Insight with your head and the element of air. Air by its nature is nebulous and invisible, just like our thoughts and thinking. We know that when we spend too much time thinking we can end up in the doldrums, being blown back and forth in confusion. Sometimes the wind can be with us and we experience a flow to our thoughts, and other times we are beating into the teeth of a gale and are confused. Go to an airy place and you'll notice that when you can see across a city from a tall building, or across the countryside from the top of a hill, you get a great sense of clarity. Looking at the sky inspires clear thinking. Air is always in motion and so are our brains.

Think of all the sayings associated with the head and its connection to the element of air: 'he has his head in the clouds', 'she is an airhead', 'he floats around here', 'she is very spacey'. When talking about ideas we often mention 'an idea that came out of thin air' or that we need to have some 'blue sky thinking'. It is useful to understand the connection between the element of air and the State of Insight, as this will help us to understand, recognise and therefore get into the State of Insight.

This powerful state is clearly linked to the head and specifically our brains. Thinking that is ungrounded is just mental dross or mental noise; in contrast, the State of Insight means that our thoughts help us to navigate the challenges of life.

GREAT THINKERS

Over the ages there have been many great thinkers. We know these people because of their achievements, their ingenuity and ultimately their legacy. They range from the unknown people who invented the wheel, to the builders of the pyramids in Egypt, to the likes of Leonardo da Vinci, to Gutenberg the inventor of the printing press, to Joyce and Yeats, to Robert

Boyle the 'father of chemistry' and Marie Curie the 'mother of modern physics', to people such as Seamus Heaney or Herta Müller, both awarded the Nobel Prize for Literature. All these people consistently manage(d) to maintain a State of Insight that allows(ed) them to accomplish great things. While you and I may not have the same abilities and faculties as the aforementioned, we do all have the ability, as they do (did), to choose to be in a State of Insight. Using our State of Insight we can build on the experiences of those who have gone before; by standing on the shoulders of these giants we can think and gain insights beyond our wildest dreams.

What is striking when you look at the work of the great thinkers throughout time, whether they are the great philosophers, writers, scientists or pioneers, is that their insights were usually very different or new when compared with the thinking of those around them. Remember that Galileo was placed under house arrest for the rest of his life by the pope as punishment for having the audacity to suggest that the earth went round the sun! Many of da Vinci's designs were ridiculed, yet it has recently been shown, for example, that his parachute would work. What the great thinkers show is that to be truly insightful and to be in a State of Insight you must be prepared to think differently and not to allow your thinking to be constrained by the sheep or herd mentality of homogenised thinking. Briefly, real insight takes bravery and confidence.

WIIFM? - WHAT'S IN IT FOR ME?

So why bother? Wouldn't it be easier to go with the flow and think as everyone else does? If you believed that, then you would not have bought this book. The fact that you are reading this suggests that you are prepared to think differently, and by doing so allow a State of Insight to prevail that will see you achieve your goals and create huge success in your life. Engaging with the State of Insight will allow you to:

- Be able to ask the right questions at the right time.
- Quickly identify information, tools and techniques for success.
- Weigh up and process information in a streamlined manner.
- Be ABC – Accurate, Brief and Concise – in your communication.
- Create a personalised learning style.

While all the benefits of the State of Insight are alluring, the one I believe forms the basis for lasting success, rather than simply 'quick wins', is the ability to create an intelligent personalised learning style. You are unique, and no other person on the planet has a brain wired exactly as yours is. This means that while some general learning styles, templates and methods can be employed, your greatest strength will grow from developing these systems to suit you, and in a way that matches your neurological and psychological framework. Remember that every system, tool or insight I present to you here must at some stage be made your own. This will mean experimenting, playing and practising to hone and perfect each technique so that it becomes your own. In doing this you will develop my work and move beyond me, and collectively we will start to create a legacy, just as those who have gone before us have done for us. By doing this your mastery of the State of Insight becomes more than just a tool for your success, but something that can help many, many more people.

PUTTING IT INTO PRACTICE

The first step in realising the ability you have to deliver clear insights is to create the right conditions or environment to allow the full extent of your abilities to unfold. So let's start now: what do you think is the most important condition to be present to allow you to be in a State of Insight?

In my opinion, it is the need to be *uninhibited* in your thinking. So what inhibits your thinking? I come across three major barriers to delivering great insights on a regular basis:

- Your perceptions – do you make mistakes or perform experiments?
- Your comfort zones – do you strive to learn outside your area of expertise?

- Your culture – what is your level of deference/
  respect for superiors?

MISTAKES OR EXPERIMENTS?

Your perceptions, or the way in which you judge yourself, will massively affect the level of success you have in consistently achieving a State of Insight. We are taught from an early age not to make mistakes. Errors are often punished in society, education and business. This has led many people to judge the quality of their thinking on whether they 'got it right'. When Thomas Edison invented the light bulb in 1837, it was supposedly after 2,999 times of 'getting it wrong'. The true mark of Edison's ability to create a State of Insight was that he did not see these as failures or mistakes, but rather as 2,999 experiments with each insight bringing him closer to success. If Edison thought in a conventional manner he would have given up trying, but he saw his experiments bringing him in the right direction.

Bob Rotella, the famous golf guru and sports psychologist, tells the story of a college basketball star who was having an awful game. The player missed seventeen baskets in the game, but his team-mates were playing well and near the final whistle both teams were level. A technical foul was called against the opposition and any player on our player's team could take the penalty. Our player insisted on taking the penalty and scored to win the game. When Rotella asked him why, after missing so many baskets, he took the penalty, he smiled and said, 'the law of averages meant I had to score!' Again we see the same self-belief in thinking and ability that allowed Edison to succeed. The lesson for us is that tenacity and determination help to change our perceptions of what is an experiment and what is a mistake.

Being optimistic helps a person to see life as a series of experiments rather than as successes or failures. Sometimes circumstances do not work out as one would wish, but the optimist still keeps going, undaunted by what others might perceive as failure. Optimists often have the ability to look at their experiments, understand what did not work well, change their behaviour or approach and move forward, sure that the changes they made will yield success. This approach to life means that the eternal optimists by chance or design will often find *meaningful* success, as they always allow themselves to be open to opportunities of success. Pessimists on the other hand rarely see success, as their restrictive thinking will not allow them to go for the opportunities that may result in achievement. They support this thinking with the sure knowledge that they have failed in the past, so why bother!

Furthermore, as Martin Seligman says in *Learned Optimism*, pessimists are more likely to suffer from depression, have immunity problems, underachieve at work and most importantly have no pleasure in life.[3] The good news is that

---

3   Seligman, *Learned Optimism*, p. 53.

optimism can be learned and in doing so you get the opposite of all the negatives above. (Google 'Learned Optimism Test' and take the test to get a score of your optimism/pessimism.)

Exercise

Apply this to both business and personal experience.

1. Recall a past experience that you saw as a failure.
2. What lessons can you learn from it?
3. Are you applying that learning today?

THE COMFORT ZONES

To release optimism you need to be brave enough to see your mistakes as experiments. This means you must confront your fears, which starts with looking at your comfort zones – the easy and unchallenging areas you operate within. After a while, the comfort zones become boring, with no spark or excitement. The walls of comfort zones are not constructed of steel or concrete, yet they can imprison us just as effectively as they are built of fear and anxiety and usually are based on what other people would think if we did, said or acted in a manner that would not be normal for us. Your State of Insight is stifled when you live in your comfort zones. The fear that keeps us in our comfort zones is not the type of fear that tells us jumping off the top floor of a building will hurt us, it is more the psychological or perceived fear that traps us. The fear that we won't be good enough or bright enough, that we might fail, that we might make a fool of ourselves. These ego-driven fears keep us in our comfort zones and stop us learning. As Susan Jeffers says, in her book of the same title: 'feel the fear and do it anyway'. To be in a State of Insight you must conquer fear and be prepared to live outside your comfort zones. To drive yourself to push forward your thinking, even if you fear the results it may bring, is what all the great philosophers, sports people, inventors, teachers and successful people in history were prepared to do.

Exercise

Personal

- What fears make up the walls of your comfort zones?
- What can you do today that will allow you to step out of the comfort zones and into the State of Insight?

Business/team

- What are the collective fears that make up your team's comfort zones?
- What can your team or business do to step beyond these comfort zones?

Fears can be divided into two clear categories: rational and irrational. Rational fear keeps us safe; for example you will fear jumping off a cliff because it could kill you. On the other hand irrational fears – such as the fear of losing a job, not being accepted, losing control, not having money – will not kill you, but can be debilitating. A very good technique to overcome fear is to logically run the 'what if' scenario. Let's take the example of fear of losing your job. Many have this fear and it hinders top performance because operating from a place of fear rather than love is draining. It all depends on how you choose to view the world. So 'what if' you got fired? If you look at it from a negative place, you see lack of money, dole queues, house repossessions, loss of stature and face. Not a nice picture. However, looking at it from a positive place, losing your job could mean that you start the business or pursue the career you always wanted. Your house is repossessed but you learn to rent and not to have the neediness of owning property and you are now free to travel and relocate to another country if you wish. You realise that the loss of position and status frees you to be yourself and not be defined by what you do but rather by who you are! So adversity turns to opportunity. This is how winners see the world.

Another technique often used in NLP (neuro-linguistic programming) is to deprogramme the negative emotional associations with the image of the fear. If you take fear of flying: start with a mental image of a plane crashing in big brilliant colour, with stereo sound on a big screen in a cinema. This would probably be a 10 on the terror scale of the person with the irrational fear. Now turn the film into black and white: the intensity drops to 8 on the scale. Then turn off the sound: now we go to 6 on the terror scale. Now shrink the movie to a TV set size: it's not so scary and maybe a 4 on the scale. Next play cartoon music as background: now we are at 2 on the scale. Finally, shrink the whole thing to the size of a dot and turn off the sound, then see the dot evaporate and disappear: 0 on the scale. Using this technique of desensitising we can work on any fear.

CULTURAL CROSSES

Just as your attitude to your mistakes and your comfort zones can affect the freedom of your thinking, so too can cultural aspects. Your cultural heritage gives you many benefits but every culture has its crosses to bear. Through working with many international companies and people, I have observed the following typical models of behaviour, which are not exclusive to each culture and I do not wish to generalise. In fact, all the models can apply at different times to a person, team or business from any background. What is important is to recognise where you or your team or your company or organisation is at. Then, using your State of Insight, you will be able to navigate the cultural hurdles.

These crosses or hurdles also define the level of ease with which you enter the State of Insight. If the typical behavioural model of a culture like Ireland or the UK is 'begrudgery' or 'tall poppy syndrome', then this environment inhibits insight. The 'tall poppy syndrome' dictates that all should grow to the same height and if one rises above the rest (or succeeds) then it should be cut back down to size. How often do we see the media and others in our own circle revel in trying to bring down progressive and insightful thinking? The reason that 'tall poppy syndrome' or 'begrudgery' exists is because when people rise above the comfort zone of others, it makes them uncomfortable as their lack of drive, innovation and insight is highlighted and they do not want this! This is never more evident than with groups of teenagers, where being the same as everyone else means social acceptance.

If you come from an Asian/Middle Eastern background that espouses traditional values of respect for elders, religion and authority, then this behavioural model can manifest itself in deference to others in authority, which can stifle the State of Insight. A friend of mine who got a great job with a Korean electronics manufacturer learned this point the hard way. He was called to a meeting with his boss and some visiting management from Korea. John (not his real name) sat at his boss's left-hand side, warmly greeted the guests and proceeded to talk enthusiastically about product innovation, behaviour that in Europe or America would be seen as go-ahead and upbeat. After the meeting, John was told never to sit to his boss's left and never to speak first in a meeting. John felt his ability to be insightful was compromised and left the company soon after. So ask yourself the following: do I defer to authority rather than share my insights? Am I overly respectful to the extent that I do not contribute enough? Or do I stifle insight by my requirement for others to defer to me?

If you come from an American or a Canadian background, the typical model is that you will usually speak up, as it is part of this model to expect input from everyone – a culture where the best and brightest are celebrated rather than sneered at. However, this can also lead to problems. Quantity does not necessarily mean quality. As somebody from this background, your challenge may be to take a 'less is more' approach. Rather than simply fill space, can you hone your thinking and insights to a degree that when you share them, they are of such a high quality that others stop and listen?

In the typical European model, the State of Insight can be restricted by a culture of politics. Being closely bunched with many political neighbours the countries of Europe, who started two world wars, have found a need to be very politically aware. This manifests as a behaviour that is based on achieving your own agenda but in doing so playing a game to keep your neighbours happy, knowing all the while that they too are playing the same game! The European Union seeks homogenisation, but also seeks to preserve uniqueness.

Being unable to truly express how you think and feel means that your insight may be subject to endless dialogue, hinting, posturing and meetings that always have a subcurrent political agenda. If you suffer this behavioural trait, the fastest way to overcome it is to stop playing the game. Call it as it is. Share your insights and in doing so others will be encouraged to share theirs.

Remember all behaviours, hurdles, crosses and lessons to learn can apply to all of us from all cultures.

Exercise
Personal
- Make a list of any cultural/societal behaviours that stop you expressing your true insights.

Business/team
- Does your team or business suffer any cultural traits that would inhibit insightful thinking?

NEURAL NETWORKS

As noted earlier one of the keys to creating lasting success is to identify your personal learning style. This is formed by a combination of nature, the aptitude with which you were born, and nurture, skills and abilities that form over time because of your interests and the people and methods to which you are exposed. There is little you can do about the nature you were born with, these aspects of ourselves tend to be hard-wired. For example, if you have a high sense of urgency and speed about you then you probably always had and always will have. You can temper this need for speed with maturity and patience, which can be learned, but your natural way will be inclined towards speed rather than a methodical regularised pace. The opportunity for accelerated learning or deep insight is provided by the aspect of your personal learning style that is influenced by nurture. By exposing yourself to the right methods and techniques, you can complement your natural skill set.

To do this in the most efficient manner we must first explore the world of neural networks. The average human brain has about 100 billion neurons and each one is connected to about 1,000 others. Think about it as being like a massive road network with primary roads, secondary roads, tertiary roads and then a series of laneways and dirt tracks. Every time a neuron fires, an electrical impulse travels from one part of the brain to another and a chemical pathway or route is established. Peptides, a form of amino acid or protein, make what are called neurotransmitters. These peptides are laid down in the brain when we think, process information, walk, talk and so on, forming routes and pathways. This is how we learn and develop automatic skills. The networks are important to the State of Insight, as by understanding how these neural networks form we realise that we can choose to think in any way we want.

Imagine a field of grass in summertime. It is lush and uniform across the field. This is like our brain before we learn something new. One day we decide to take a walk in the field; by doing this we leave a faint trail in the grass. This is the equivalent of learning something for the first time where a faint chemical path is laid down. The following day we decide to walk across the field again, but the track we left previously is so faint we cannot find it so we take another route. Another faint pathway is created. Day three and we come back again but this time we find the first trail we made and follow it. Now a much more pronounced and embedded trail develops. If for two more weeks we walk the same trail, we find that it forms a clear path and is now very easy to find. Learning is similar, the more we do something the more we create routes and pathways in our brain. In time the pathway becomes so familiar as to become an automatic route that no longer needs conscious thought.

Some pathways will be easy to create because the meadow is lush. Nature has predisposed us to these skills. Other pathways must be made across broken ground and these are harder to establish but over time can be very clear. These are the skills we have to develop by repetition. For example, when you first learn to drive you have to think about your actions:

change gears, use your mirrors and so on. Once these actions are repeated hundreds of times the neural pathways become established and we no longer need to actively think about driving, it has become automatic.

The concept of neural networks explains why we can find it so difficult to change our behaviour: the old road is there and so is easy to follow. The new road or new behaviour needs to be built, so requires more work. Many cognitive behavioural therapists believe that it takes twenty-one days to form these new pathways or new behaviours. So, as the old adage goes, 'practice makes perfect'. The same is true of cluttered and confused thinking: the more you do it the more deeply ingrained it becomes. The State of Insight needs to be practised and the more we allow ourselves to think with insight the easier it becomes.

TOOLS AND TECHNIQUES

There are literally thousands of techniques and tools that will help you to improve your brainpower. They are based on the principle that your brain is like a muscle and must be exercised, given the right levels of nutrition and rest. Think of brain tools as being like a gym for the mind and training aids that will allow your brain to perform great tasks when required. We would expect Olympic athletes to train for years before their chosen event, yet we expect our brains to be at their best often without any training. To help train your mind we can look at some tools. I have selected three that I have found make an incredible difference to people training their brain to consistently create a State of Insight:

1. Creative association – 'all things are connected'.
2. Mind maps – a sympathetic system of recreating neural networks.
3. Visualisation – unlocking the power of the RAS (reticular awareness system).

1. Creative association

Leonardo da Vinci, one of the greatest thinkers of all time, is known to have been fuelled by the curiosity brought to mind by his motto 'all things are connected'. The technique of creative association is very useful as it teaches our brain to allow new connections to be made between seemingly disparate pieces of information; that is, the ability to create insight. Some notable examples of the result of such insights include the Post-IT and the Sony Walkman. The Post-IT was developed when paper company 3M set out to design some paper glue for office and home use. To their dismay, they found that the glue did not work permanently, although it did seem to retain a low level of stickiness. Instead of giving up, the 3M people asked a question – 'what can people do with sticky paper?' – and found they had created a whole new product, which today is still a bestseller. The Sony Walkman came about not by looking for a new technology but by taking already existing components, namely a tape deck and headphones, and combining them in a new way for a new use based upon music on the move.

Anybody can be creative, and by making a conscious decision to be in a State of Insight, you will be. As the process by which insight occurs is as subconscious as it is conscious, the following exercise will help develop your brain's ability to create insight.

Exercise

Step 1

- Pick a question that you or your team would like the answer to or a problem that you or your team would like to solve. Write it down. For example, How do I create success in my life?

Step 2

- Make a list of twenty random words. For example:

Purple	Knife	Candle	Picture	CD
People	Light	Water	Orange	Cushion
Book	Penny	Ball	Buddha	The Rolling Stones
Flashing	Sonic	Glass	Message	Volcano

Step 3

- Pick ten words from the list that you can associate in some way to the question you have posed. For example:

1. A *knife* to cut through confusion.
2. Get a big *picture* view.
3. Read some *books* to get help.
4. Look after my *pennies* and the pounds will count themselves.
5. Shed some *light* on my blind spots to see what is stopping me.
6. Know I have the potential energy of a *volcano*.
7. Ask other *people* for advice.
8. Do I have a safety *cushion* that I am attached to?
9. What is my *message* to others?
10. If I look in the looking *glass*, who and what do I see?

Step 4

- Cross off your list the ten words you chose and you get a new list:

Purple	Candle	CD	Water
Orange	Ball	Buddha	Flashing
Sonic	The Rolling Stones		

Step 5

- From the remaining ten words, pick five that you can in some way associate with your question. For example:

1. *Water* can carry us to new places, lands and ideas.
2. Be like a *ball* and roll easy.
3. Take action like a *sonic* boom and shock myself into thinking in a new way.
4. Make sure that I do not 'burn the *candle* at both ends' and instead find balance in my life.
5. Listen to a motivational or meditation *CD*.

Step 6

- Now cross the five words you used off the list and you get your final list. From the remaining five words, construct a sentence or use those words to find the solution to your problem. Remember that all things are connected. For example:

How do I create success in my life?

Purple Orange Buddha Flashing The Rolling Stones

- Buddha is not only the name of a man but also a term used to describe people who have achieved a state of enlightenment. Part of my journey is to find enlightenment in small areas and to share these insights with other people. Oranges are a great source of Vitamin C, and to help me to be successful I must maintain and increase my vitality and sourcing fresh food will help this. Flashing lights draw attention, how can I make my words flashing lights so that people will interact with my work and benefit from it? Purple is a colour that unites blue and red, the colours of masculine and feminine energy. By uniting these aspects of my own self, I will achieve balance and success. A rolling stone gathers no moss. Movement, excitement and getting out of my comfort zone will make sure that I continually grow and do not go stale.

Or

- I can imagine that my success will have all the energy of a Rolling Stones concert, with flashing purple and orange lights, but behind it all, I will be serene and contented like a Buddha!

What happens in this exercise is that your brain is forced to stretch and make connections in unusual ways, going beyond the obvious to open up new neural networks to access new areas of your brain. The mind has amazing plasticity and can make connections between highly disparate elements, yet unite them all in a common purpose. This exercise is very good for connecting the left and right hemispheres of the brain as it requires both creativity and logic. The more you do this exercise the deeper and more fascinating the insights you will uncover into the question you are using the technique with.

A very similar way of thinking led to this book. I was lying in bed very early one morning and the general idea of this book was circulating in my brain. I knew that there was a vehicle that could hold all my thoughts, knowledge and experience gained from helping people to create success. As I lay in bed thinking about this I noticed my Nike AIR tennis shoe reflecting in the mirror, then my glass of WATER beside me, then the FIRE rays of the morning sun coming in the window and then the physical space I was in that was constructed from materials of the EARTH. This line of thinking led me to a moment of inspiration and a State of Insight where I could see that each of the **5 States of Success** – Insight, Connection, Certainty, Vitality and Spirit – were linked to the five elements: air, water, earth, fire and ether. These five states could then be linked to our physical beings: the head, the heart, the gut, the whole physical body and the animating force of life.

You can use the creative association technique to find inspiration on a question that you are stuck on or you can use it as a brainstorming tool to find new ways of thinking about the same things. In doing this you will invoke your State of Insight.

2. Mind mapping

Neither of my books would have been completed without the use of mind maps. Mind mapping is a technique pioneered by Tony Buzan. Its brilliance is in its simplicity. You remember I mentioned neural networks and the fact that our minds are like a series of road networks, with pieces of information connecting to other pieces: mind mapping mirrors the way in which our brains work. Most of us when we put information into a computer or on a page do so in list-based or linear format. Yet our brains store information over a network not unlike a spider's web, and a huge proportion of information in our brains is stored in visual format. Think about all the people's faces you know but you do not remember their names.

You may have played this game with friends or family: a player places an imaginary item in an imaginary suitcase and as each person takes a turn he or she adds another item, so you could find, 'in the suitcase I packed a toothbrush, a mop, a squirrel, a Ferrari, a jade ring, a jumper, a pair of shoes' and so on. The aim of the game is to remember as many items as possible. Watch the next time you play this game, after six or seven items the person recalling will lose focus from their eyes and go searching in their brain for the next item. You could almost leave the room and they would not be aware of it. This presents a very interesting insight into how we store and recall information. Three things become clear about how our brains store and process information:

1. We struggle to store information in a linear manner.

2. We have very high recall of imagery.

3. Recalling too many linear items makes us lose our awareness and connectedness to those around us.

To overcome these limitations we can use mind maps.

Exercise

Construct a mind map. The best way to understand mind maps is to do one. Follow the steps below and look at the example as well.

1. Get a sheet of paper and some coloured pens.

2. Turn the page to landscape format.

3. In the centre of the page, write your question or subject matter.

4. Add a symbol, logo or image associated with your question.

5. Draw a minimum of five branches out from the centre, writing a topic along each.

6. From the topic, draw smaller branches with connected thoughts or details.

7. Add pictures, shading or other graphic elements.

On the next page is a mind map of the **5 States of Success**, which was used to help plan the structure of this book. It contains over fifty elements, with each element being a topic for discussion in the book. Each of these elements in turn has other mind maps where it becomes the central piece of information and another mind map begins.[4]

This is a remarkable technique for planning, memorising, decluttering your thoughts and coming up with new ideas. It puts you firmly into a State of Insight. When running a workshop in the UK for a group of accountants who were used to dealing with information in a linear manner I did a test of the mind map. As a group, we constructed a mind map with over seventy individual items. We looked at the mind map for five minutes and then broke for lunch for an hour. On our return, I asked the group to reconstruct the mind map unaided. When they were satisfied after ten minutes that they had recreated the mind map we put the original up beside the recreated version and to the amazement of all involved they were identical! The group were staggered by what they could recall in such a short time. Could you memorise a list of seventy items in under five minutes and recall them one hour later in less than ten minutes? I suspect without a mind map or similar technique you would struggle or not be able to complete the task. Test this, try it for yourself.

---

4   Created using ThinkBuzan's iMindMap, see www.thinkbuzan.com.

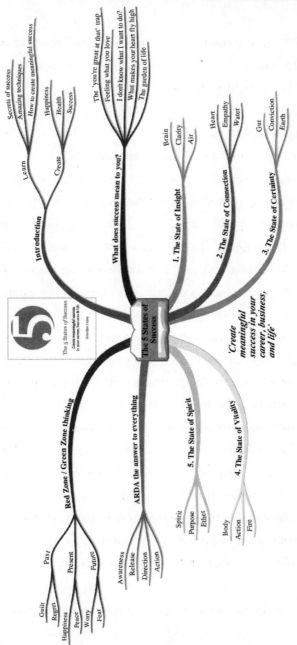

For more information on mind maps visit *www.thinkbuzan.com* or get yourself a copy of *The Mind Map Book* by Tony and Barry Buzan.

3. Visualisation

Of all the techniques I use with clients and use myself, the power of visualisation is not to be underestimated. When we visualise a course of action or a positive result some very interesting things happen in our physiology and neurology. First a part of the brain called the RAS or reticular awareness system becomes activated. The RAS helps regulate our waking and sleeping states and serves as a filter to allow us to navigate a world where we encounter millions of stimuli. Your RAS works like a radar. In a ship you can set the radar to pick up different objects by size, by movement or by distance. In the same way we can programme the RAS to bring into our awareness that which we desire.

Have you ever noticed, when you have changed a car, how many other cars of the same type are already out there? Yet before you owned your new car you were not aware of these others. When we visualise what we want in our lives we become 'on the look out' for aspects associated with these goals or objectives. For instance if you want to create a State of Insight you will start to notice people who are very insightful, you will notice books and articles that refer to insight, you will remember tools or experiences that will support you in creating insights.

What also happens when we visualise positive scenarios or happenings is that we associate very positive feelings of well-being and happiness with that vision. This serves to relax the body by releasing hormones such as serotonin and endorphins which make us feel good and increase our ability to take action and think clearly. The combination of these hormones and the focus created by being cognisant of what you want in your life puts you in the best possible position to achieve the results that you want. I am convinced that visualisation activates parts of the brain that we do not fully understand and that these produce an 'X' factor that seems to help people to produce dramatic results, driven as much by the subconscious as the conscious.

Visualisation works best when the brain goes into an alpha state. When alpha brain waves are created (8–12 Hz), we can visualise easily and become very receptive to information; it is a very relaxed but aware state. You may experience alpha waves watching TV, meditating or when in the 'zone'. When you are in a lucid dream state you also experience alpha waves. An experiment by Australian psychologist Alan Richardson showed the power of visualisation in a very dramatic way. He selected a group of basketball players none of whom had ever practised visualisation before. He broke them into three further groups: group a) who practised shooting baskets for twenty minutes each day for a month; group b) who practised shooting baskets every day ONLY by visualising; and group c) who had neither actual practice nor visualisation. Both the players who practised actual shots and those who visualised the shots showed the same improvement, which shows that we can create a state of success or insight even before we undertake the task or challenge at hand. The players who did not practise showed no improvement.[5]

Visualising in advance of a speech, a race, a job interview, a game, an important meeting, a first date, to be thin, to stop smoking, to be brilliant or in fact in any area in which you wish to improve, will hugely increase your chance of success. A by-product of visualisation is the development of confidence, as through visualisation you will feel that you have already conquered your challenge before you even start and therefore feel confident when you go into the actual situation.

One of the best ways to visualise is to listen to a guided mediation/visualisation. You can download a free visualisation audio track from my website at www.the5statesofsuccess.com or www.brendanfoley.net, or purchase the audio CD from the same location. Alternatively, you can follow the process below:

Exercise

Visualisation. Create a vision of what you want in your life or for your team. A team member could read this while the rest of the group participates in the exercise.

---

5   See www.livestrong.com/article/94767-mental-training-basketball/

1. Lower the lights and preferably play soft music very low that does not have any lyrics. Something soothing is best. Make sure the room temperature is comfortable and that you will not be disturbed.

2. Sit with your legs and arms uncrossed, or lie flat on your back.

3. Close your eyes and become aware of your breathing. Notice how it comes and goes. Notice how it feels warmer as you breathe out and cooler as you breathe in.

4. Take a deep breath, expand your belly and hold for three seconds, now breathe out deeply, fully emptying your lungs. Repeat this twice more.

5. Allow your breathing to move to a natural pace and rhythm that is comfortable for you. Allow your body to relax, feeling any stress, strain or tightness leave your muscles.

6. Feel that every breath you take allows you to go deeper and deeper into a highly relaxed, but aware, state. Feel that any worries, anxiety or stress are washing away with each breath that you take.

7. Imagine, sense or see a bright light above your head. Let this light intensify in brightness. Feel it drop down and touch your scalp and instantly

feel the muscles in your scalp relax. Feel the light continue down, relaxing as it goes: relax your brain, your brow, your eyes, your eyelids, your ears, your jaw, your tongue, your gums, your throat, the back of your neck, the sides of your neck. Feel light flow down your arms, your elbows, your forearms and your wrists and hands all the way to the tips of your fingers. Let the light come down your shoulders, relaxing your collar bones, your upper back, your chest, your middle back, your abdomen, your lower back, your hips and pelvis, your groin, your thighs, your hamstrings and your knees, back and front. Feel the light go down your calves and shins to your ankles, feet and toes. You are now totally covered in relaxing light and feel great. All the time your breathing is bringing you deeper and deeper into a state of relaxation.

8. Visualise a beautiful room with a large window at one end. Walk to this window. Outside, you see yourself or your team achieving what you want to achieve. Notice the colours. What are people/you wearing? What are they/you saying? What are they/you doing? How are they/you feeling? Notice all the sounds that are there. Notice all the movements. Notice the expressions on people's/your face(s). Notice their/your body language.

9. Allow the brightness of the colours to increase.

Allow the sounds to increase. Allow the feelings of success and achievement to increase. Allow the window to grow bigger so that everyone seems bigger and closer. See yourself or your team achieving everything that you wish for. See yourself or your team receiving accolades and feel the huge sense of happiness all around.

10. Allow yourself to fly through the window and merge with the you outside. Feel how wonderful it is to be achieving these great things. Feel how happy and satisfied you are, how aware and how insightful. Now allow these feelings to intensify. You are almost overwhelmed by the feelings of happiness and satisfaction and achievement.

11. Know that you are creating the reality that you want, and know that you can come back to this place any time you want to connect with these feelings and visualise your success.

12. Slowly come back into the room with the window. Become aware of your physical body. Ask your brain to remember the great feelings of success that you felt. Become aware of your breathing again. Take a deep breath in and release. Repeat twice.

13. Keeping your eyes closed, wriggle your toes and fingers. Take another deep breath in and open your eyes feeling refreshed and energised.

This is a wonderful tool to use as a team or an individual and to build neural networks that are connected to feelings of success which will allow your RAS and subconscious to deliver effortless success.

ICONS OF THINKING

Modelling is a well-known technique in coaching and training. It works on the basis that many other people before you have faced the same challenge that you face today. Many of these predecessors came up with methods to overcome that challenge and in observing them and their methods we can often fast-track our learning. In studying these people, we start to recognise characteristics in ourselves that will allow us to achieve similar feats, or to use our abilities in similar ways.

Within the scope of the State of Insight you may seek clarity in your logical thinking, in your creative thought process or in communicating clearly. You can be guaranteed that there is somebody sitting close to you now who will have experienced a challenge in one of these three areas and has conquered this challenge. In deciding who to model our methods on, it is very important that the person is inspiring to you. I have listed some great thinkers under the headings of logic, creativity and clarity. Google them, get their biographies and above all then ask the question, what would 'X' think if 'X' was in my shoes?

For example, what would Leonardo da Vinci think if he were here now? How would he approach this challenge?

- *Logic:* Garry Kasparov, Leonardo da Vinci, Naomi Wolf, Albert Einstein, Friedrich Nietzsche, Bill Gates, Marie Curie, David McWilliams.

- *Creativity:* Pablo Picasso, Maeve Binchy, Lady Gaga, James Dyson, Nina Simone, Salvador Dali, Damien Hirst, Dylan Thomas, Colm Tóibín, John B. Keane.

- *Clarity and communication:* Barack Obama, Bill Clinton, Oprah Winfrey, Martin Luther King, Miriam O'Callaghan, Bono, Mary Robinson.

You may also know people not on the lists who you are inspired by in terms of their thinking. What would they think? When you access this type of thinking using this method of modelling, you are awakening archetypal patterns in your subconscious. Archetypes are personality patterns that have been repeated throughout the ages and you see them in every drama, film, story and all around you. In keeping with this vein of thinking, you may be invoking within yourself the archetype of the artist or inventor in terms of creativity. You may be invoking the archetype of the scientist or philosopher in terms of logic or you may be calling upon the internal personality traits you have that echo them in terms of creating clarity and communicating your thinking.

The most important aspect of creating the State of Insight is just to do it. Use the techniques of mind mapping, visualisation and modelling outlined above, play with them, and make up your own. One of my favourite quotations, from Oliver Wendell Holmes, captures the benefits of the State of Insight: 'Once the horizons of the mind have been expanded they can never again return to where they once were.'

SUMMARY

**Key attribute: State of Insight =
Clarity to combine logic and creativity**

Memory trigger: Head, Air

- We are living in an unprecedented time defined by unlimited access to information, and success is about using that information in the best way we can, both logically and creatively.

- From Leonardo da Vinci to Marie Curie we have seen that great thinkers refuse to make mistakes; instead they perform experiments or learn lessons.

- Cultural crosses and comfort zones limit our thinking and our potential, but we can use our neural networks to empower our minds and create clarity.

- Using mind mapping, visualisation and creative associations we explored the wonderful world of innovative thinking that delivers the raw material to allow us to create clarity and communication.

- Be brave! Try new things, help to evolve your own mind, the minds of your team and your business, and in doing so you are helping to continue the journey of the last 200,000 years that has seen your amazing brain become what it is today – a masterpiece!

Here is a word cloud of the most common words in this section. The larger the word the more common it is. By looking at these key words it will help you to recall the subject matter and get a mental snapshot of what you have read.

Part 2 –
The State of Connection

The State of Connection – creates _EMPATHY_
- Builds relationships
- Promotes emotional intelligence
- Develops teamwork
- Memory trigger: your heart, element of water

By the very fact that we are human, we all seek connections with others. Community and teamwork are hard-wired in us from our evolutionary journey over the last 200,000 years. When we connect with other people we form relationships and relationships are the currency of human achievement.

When we form a relationship, whether it is good or bad, we are learning about others through empathy – the ability to see, sense, feel or experience what life is like from the perspective of the other person. Some of the most successful people in the world have an average IQ (Intelligence Quotient) but almost all have an excellent EQ (Emotional Quotient or Emotional Intelligence).

Most successful people in life, business and sport demonstrate the State of Connection and have the power and ability to build and forge relationships based on their empathy and emotional intelligence. Great businesses or organisations are no different in that they too build great relationships with their customers. Having the ability to create relationships allows you to connect to people who have skills beyond yours and in different fields. This in turn allows you to leverage their skills and they can leverage yours, and in this way we form the practical basis for teamwork.

It is also through the State of Connection that we find personally satisfying relationships and inspirational and uplifting people. We are all a mixture of introvert and extrovert personalities. Those who are mostly introverted are self-motivated and those who are extroverted are motivated by the buzz or energy of the people around them. Everyone has some extrovert qualities and these require the stimulation of others. Even if you are a person with low extrovert levels, you will need validation or empowerment from others at some stage, and if you are very extrovert, relationships will be your fuel and you will need them as your sustenance.

To be in a State of Connection is to be able to share the emotion of a dream, vision or reality with other people so that they may benefit from your experience and insights, and in return for you to be able to empathise with their dreams, visions and ideas.

WATER AND EMOTION

As with the State of Insight, which as an *aide-mémoire* or memory trigger we connected to the element of air, the State of Connection can be expressed through the element of water. Water, like emotions, can exist in many states: as ice, emotions can be unmoving, cold and stubborn, refusing to budge; as steam, emotions can be hot-headed and powerful but evaporate very quickly; as liquid, emotions can be flowing and easy. Water, like emotions, can never be fully contained and, like emotions, will always find a way out. Even the greatest dam in the world will give way to erosion. People who are very emotional can be as gentle as the ripple on a lake or as devastating as stormy waters.

The greatest metaphor water can provide, I believe, is that ultimately it connects all life: there is no life without water. Remember that all life on earth emerged from the sea. Water connects everything and whether by trade, by sea or by biology it is the linking element to all living things. In terms of the State of Connection, everyone is programmed to send and receive emotion and this ultimately builds our relationships.

When you wish to be in a State of Connection, imagine you are a wave and all others you meet are other waves. All the waves are living in the ocean of emotion. Some waves you will clash with, some you will roll with, some will be gentle, others strong, but ultimately you and every other wave are made of the same ocean and because of that you can empathise with anybody.

HEARTS AND MINDS

Just as water is symbolic of the nature of connection, so is the heart. When we see a heart shape we think of love, beauty, friendship, courage and so on. It represents not our physical heart but the metaphorical heart that is the most central and intimate point of our emotional being. Pure connection, joy and happiness stem from it. When we allow our hearts to connect to those of others, we form incredible bonds and relationships. Most happy and successful people will value their relationships as their most prized possessions. From the romantic and passionate connection of lovers, to the highest concept of the soulmate type of companionship, to the unconditional love of a parent for a child, to the warm camaraderie of team-mates and colleagues, these aspects give us a sense of warmth and belonging. According to Ram Dass, the spiritual writer and guru, many studies show that when people are at the end of their lives it is never money, status or power that they look fondly back on, it is the relationships that they formed and the difference that they made in the world that they value most highly.

Many expressions have come across the ages to capture the essence of the nature of the heart: 'she's all heart' to describe somebody committed and passionate; 'a brave heart' to describe someone of stout courage. When people feel real joy, they describe it as 'heartfelt'. The heart in its metaphorical state is essentially our happiness and our sense of self. A big bank balance without a happy heart is of little consolation. The true feelings of our hearts are often unknown to us until we encounter others we admire or who inspire us. In this moment we are experiencing an image of ourselves, for what we tend to love and admire in others, we love and admire in ourselves. This is why motivation can never be created from the head, it has to come from the heart. To motivate others you have to shine the light on what they really love and in this way great achievements can take place. Hence the phrase used when trying to persuade or manage people that you must appeal to 'hearts and minds'.

If you look at some of the most successful people of our time, especially in political life, their success is, and was, based on rousing people's hearts, not their minds. From Winston

Churchill to Gandhi, Aung San Suu Kyi, Benazir Bhutto, Nelson Mandela, John F. Kennedy, John Hume, Mary Robinson and Barack Obama, all these leaders demonstrate(d) a charisma, presence and aura that connects to the heart of people. Their skill as leaders was, and is, knowing that when you speak with passion and from the heart, words become empowering and uplifting.

The world of sport is no different, or the worlds of art or science. People who top their fields speak with such passion and infectious energy that they inspire many more to follow their example and to create even greater achievements than they have. So ask yourself, do you speak from your heart with passion? Do you connect with people through the things that you love? Do you show bravery in saying and sharing what is really in your heart, even if this will 'rock the boat'? Do you look forward with relish to creating new relationships and connecting with people who will inspire you, and you them? And most of all do you connect with your own heart?

IN THE BEGINNING

We are programmed by evolution to operate in communities. From the earliest days of our ancestors, it was realised that our strength together far outweighed our individual strength and we came together in tribes. We also realised that some people were better at teaching, others at hunting, others at making, others at cooking and so on. By combining our talents as a team, group or tribe we maximised our chances of success and ultimately survival. Over history, we have learned that as a people we can work well together and achieve more in this manner, which is where civilisation springs from. Research has shown that these meaningful relationships are limited to a finite number. The findings of Robin Dunbar, a British anthropologist, show that 150 is the average number of people found in tribes or villages all over the world. His hypothesis is that 150 is the maximum number of quality relationships that a human can handle. After this number, people become acquaintances rather than people we can hold a meaningful relationship with. It also explains why we let go of some relationships, as we require the room to let in new people.

The implications for businesses are that companies and organisations with over 150 employees cannot create effective relationships between them all. The number in real terms is even smaller if we take family and friends into account before our work colleagues. I would estimate about fifty to seventy as the maximum number of working relationships we can have. In terms of business planning, this means that a large company should have a maximum of fifty in a business unit to optimise the relationships and teamwork. This then provides the organisation with an emotionally intelligent structure that can be flexible and effective without needing a litany of processes and procedures. Do not fear if you work in a structure larger than this, if you allow the empathic or limbic brain to do its work you should be able to instantly create a working relationship with almost anyone.

SOCIAL MEDIA - AN EXTENSION OF THE BRAIN

I believe that the limited number of 'real relationships' we can hold has coincided with the amazing advances in Internet technology to produce an extension of our brain. It would be impossible to remember the details, interests and news of all our friends and acquaintances just using the brain alone. With the development of social media, we can see an instant solution to this problem. With the click of a mouse, we can see everything that a friend, family member or acquaintance has been up to on their Facebook page or Twitter profile. From a business perspective, websites such as LinkedIn and Plaxo give us regular updates on people and companies in our business network. These technologies allow us to focus on the 'real relationships' with our own mind power, but we achieve the best of both worlds by also staying in contact with a wide network of friends, colleagues and acquaintances.

It will be interesting to observe the generation growing up with social media networking as their main tool of interaction and to see how this affects the skill of empathy and therefore the ability to create a State of Connection. I suspect the empathy that has taken 200,000 years to develop will struggle to compete with modern technology and so we must be vigilant with our children, teams and businesses that virtual reach to many does not outweigh the need to be skilful at empathising.

THE CONNECTOR'S BRAIN

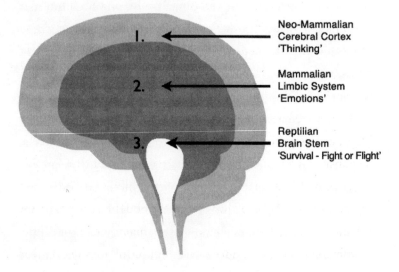

We have three main parts to our brains from the perspective of evolution:

1. the reptilian brain
2. the mammalian brain
3. the neo-mammalian brain

The reptilian brain is based above our spinal cord and is the most primal part of the brain, being one of the earliest parts to have developed in our evolutionary cycle. It has a very simple function: survival. It makes decisions that will keep us alive by choosing fight, flight or freeze. It is very primal and basic, and is seen in the nature of many reptile carnivores who hunt alone rather than in socially organised packs or groups.

Wrapped around the reptilian brain is the limbic or mammalian brain. Its function is based around connecting to others. Many mammals, in contrast to most reptiles, work as herds, pods, packs, troops or social groups. This part of the human brain is responsible for relationships and emotion.

Finally we have the cerebral cortex or the neo-mammalian brain, covering both the limbic and the reptilian brain. It is responsible for thinking and we share this thinking brain with other primates, elephants, whales and dolphins. It is the part of the brain capable of independent thought and problem-solving. Taken together, the reptilian, mammalian and neo-mammalian brains produce a very powerful combination of skills.

Within our brains, the limbic system or mammalian brain dictates our emotions and hence is where the State of Connection resides. Our brains, when under stress, stop us being in a State of Connection and empathising with others. We need to understand that the reptilian brain is the home of the 'fight or flight' response and if we are stressed, angry or fearful we cannot form or manage relationships effectively. For example, picture a sales director who might lose her bonus chastising a sales rep about a poor quarter, but not trying to empathise with the rep to find out why sales were poor. How often do you see someone else's point of view when you are angry?

Likewise if we are locked into our thinking brains or the cerebral cortex (neo-mammalian) brain, then we cannot get beyond our thoughts and form meaningful relationships with others. Imagine a financial director poring over spreadsheets and figures, and a junior accountant requesting help with an issue. The director says 'not now, ask me later … I'm busy' and at the same time fails to see the nervous disposition and stress on the face of the junior and so no empathy comes into play. The junior now becomes even more stressed having been knocked back by the director. In the future the junior will be very slow to ask for his help, leading to poor communication, a lack of trust and an unmotivated employee. All this could have been avoided by empathising and recognising, by the body language, that the person really needed a helping hand.

Have you ever been so consumed in a mental task that you misread what another person was trying to communicate?

Those two examples are not born out of ill will but out of a lack of awareness and a failure to understand and value empathy. As we will see, everybody has the ability to create empathy using mirror neurons.

MIRROR NEURONS AND EMPATHY

We all instinctively wish to be seen for what is good in us and to connect to what is good and great in others. This desire or biological programming to connect with other people came startlingly to light in 1996 with the publication of research from an Italian team led by Giacomo Rizzolatti.[6]

While monitoring the brains of monkeys, his team observed a remarkable thing. When monkey 'A' reached for a nut, a part of its brain became active, and in monkey 'B', watching monkey 'A', the same part of its brain lit up even though it did not move. This was seen again when a researcher reached for a nut: the monkey's brain activity lit up, even though it had not moved. The 'mirror neuron' had been found.

Subsequent experiments with humans revealed the same phenomenon. As Dr Marco Iacoboni, a neuroscientist from the University of California, states: 'if you see me choke up, in emotional distress from striking out at home plate [a baseball term for being knocked out without scoring], mirror neurons in your brain simulate my distress. You automatically have empathy for me. You know how I feel because you literally feel what I am feeling.'[7]

Our mirror neurons power and drive empathy. Having empathy with another person is a very powerful way to build

---

6 Miller, 'Neuroscience: reflecting on another's mind', pp. 945–947.

7 Blakeslee, 'Cells that read minds'.

emotional bridges and is a key indicator of somebody who is in a State of Connection. When someone empathises with us, we no longer feel alone and the concept of real teamwork comes into play. When we feel that someone is listening and understands us, it can be liberating, particularly when we are challenged by something that overwhelms our ability to cope. As psychologist Carl Rogers said, 'When a person realises he has been deeply heard, his eyes moisten. I think in some real sense, he is weeping for joy. It is as though he were saying "Thank God, somebody heard me. Somebody knows what it is like to be me".'[8]

I have been fortunate to experience a deep type of empathy where I have felt that my entire being has been witnessed and understood. Not in a way of being judged but more in a way of being honoured. Because of these experiences it is something I actively practice, especially in coaching sessions where sometimes just by witnessing, empathising and therefore honouring someone's story or experience, amazing and cathartic emotional and mental healing occurs. In this way a very powerful State of Connection is entered into that has the power to overcome any interpersonal obstacle.

Deep listening goes against all of our ingrained Western education and culture. We live in a world where the one who

---

8   Rogers, 'Reinhold Niebuhr's *The Self and the Dramas of History*: A criticism', pp. 15–17.

shouts the loudest is the one who is heard and the speed of life and business shuts out the opportunity for real and deep listening. When was the last time you listened to someone without judgement or without any preconceived notions or agenda of what you wished to communicate to them? Most people can do this for about a minute and then feel they either want to fix the person they are speaking with, help them, suggest something, argue a point and so on. I find that almost without exception the majority of businesses and teams I work with do not listen to each other. It is all noise but nobody is listening.

Empathy can bring us to amazing places. Take the story of Mark (not his real name), the CEO of a major international manufacturing company. Mark approached me to do some work with his marketing director who, he felt, was suffering from stress. Alana (not her real name), a very well-qualified and experienced marketing director, was achieving great results. Yet in the office she was tense, very demanding of her team and had fractious relationships with other departments in the business. Mark had seen these signs and concluded, after some conversations with Alana, that she was stressed and required outside intervention and support. He thought there must be aspects of her personal life causing the stress. When I met Alana we exchanged the usual pleasantries and I simply asked her to tell me how things were going in her life and work. As she spoke her body language suggested strain around work, rather than home, so I asked, 'What is making you stressed at work?'

Having at first denied she was stressed, she said Mark was creating uncertainty in her role. I knew, however, that Mark had earmarked Alana for a major international promotion. To really understand this I needed to go beyond the facts and uncover the underlying issue preventing good communication.

In Alana's presence I put myself into Mark's mindset and expressed, from his perspective, that I saw this promotion as a great 'pat on the back' for work well done, but that I felt dismayed that Alana was reacting so coldly to the offer and seemed to have her mind elsewhere. Alana was nearly ready to explode at this stage, saying, 'That's not the case, he is making me stressed because I don't want that job, I feel like it is a demotion and I want to stay in this country, but I don't want to tell Mark that in case he thinks I am not interested in my work.'

There it was. Both Mark and Alana had different perceptions of the role but neither had empathised with the other and both could only see the situation from their own standpoint. As Dr Wayne Dyer, the great teacher, says, '*if you change the way you look at things, then the things you look at change*'. Following our meeting, and respecting the confidentiality of the session, I asked Mark to 'really put yourself in Alana's shoes and see if you could be doing anything to stress her, and look for the big things that, if you were in her shoes, would affect you'. He suddenly realised that the promotion might not have been seen as a good thing by Alana, but actually as a sign that he did not want her as part of his team. Mark and Alana met shortly afterwards and actually listened to each other and shared their different views. A compromise was reached with Alana retaining her local role and receiving a pay increase.

The key to unravelling this issue, and almost every issue I encounter that is interpersonal, is to use empathy. Mark, Alana and I all using our empathy created the dynamic for openness. This experience will have helped to grow everyone's emotional intelligence and this is the oil in smooth teamwork. I have had the same success with sports teams, public organisations, individuals and companies and in each case the issue would not have arisen if people valued empathy more.

Exercise

Personal

- Ask yourself 'how often do I really get into a State of Connection with others so that I truly empathise with them?'

Business/team

- What level of true connection and empathy is taking place in your team?

EMOTIONAL BRIDGES

The relationships we form can be seen as emotional bridges

and are constructed through trust, openness, respect and empathy. These bridges in turn allow us to have channels of communication with each other and form an emotionally connected network of people, linked together by shared values. Stephen Covey describes this process in a very succinct and intuitive manner. He speaks of the emotional bank account each one of us has, where we make deposits and withdrawals with everyone we have a relationship with. When we compliment, empathise or empower a partner, colleague or friend, we deposit credit into their emotional bank account. When we criticise or make people feel negative about themselves, we make a withdrawal from their emotional bank account. If we only make withdrawals, then we quickly run out of credit and the relationship fails. What we always have to ask ourselves is: have we the balance right with those around us? Are you overdrawn with some people? Do you need to start making deposits into the accounts of loved ones and colleagues? Have you too much credit with others?

If we are continually overdrawn, then the emotional bridges that allow communication in our relationships break down. An atmosphere of distrust then arises and major corrective action is required to bring everyone back online. This is often when my services are called upon. I witness, most weeks, people who are struggling as teams to run businesses or find happiness because they have failed to invest in each other as real people. By treating each other as titles such as 'head' of this function, or 'vice president' of that or 'director' of this we fail to realise that emotional bridges are not built between titles, they are built between people. Many people simply misunderstand each other or lack the ability to build emotional bridges because of a lack of empathy. As the next story shows, treating people as if they can only be at their best is a marvellous way to build emotional bridges.

IF OTHERS COULD ONLY BE AT THEIR BEST

At a recent conference where I was speaking, I had an opportunity to sign and sell some of my books. Most people came straight up, purchased a book and had a quick chat. During this time I noticed a woman thumbing through the pages of my book *The Yin Yang Complex* with great interest. She looked at the back cover, then the front and put the book down. I noticed that she was drawn to pick it up again yet did not come over to me to purchase the book. Having spent many years in sales, I could see that she was interested in buying the book but something was stopping her. I struck up a conversation, and we engaged in some interesting discussion about the book and its content. She then apologised to me for taking up my time and explained that she had no money with her. I told her that she could take away the book and accompanying CD and send on a cheque to me. She protested that she did not want to do this. I repeated my offer to her and she cried and hugged me.

A little bit taken aback, I told her it was just a book and I trusted her. She then said, 'You do not know how much this means to me at this moment in my life, when so many people do not trust me. You do not know me at all, but have trusted me. Thank you so much.' And with that she left. Thinking no more of it I went on with the evening lecture and afterwards I was very surprised to see the lady there once more. She had returned with the money for the book and CD. I never found out what it was that was happening in her life and never met her again, but I do know that treating her as if she could only be at her best had a positive impact on her life.

Who could you treat as if they could only be at their best?

EMPATHY AGAINST THE ODDS

Treating people as being at their best happens when you become empathetic. I saw the State of Connection and empathy working when a friend spoke of a situation that occurred to a work colleague of hers. My friend's colleague, let's call him Andy, had just landed a major job at a rival firm of his current employers. He was delighted about his move, but his boss was not so happy when he accepted his resignation letter. When Andy went for a medical assessment as part of the formalities of joining his new company a terrible discovery was made. He had advanced cancer and would require immediate and very expensive treatment. His condition meant that the new employer rescinded their offer of employment.

Andy was now in a real predicament. He had resigned from his old employer, which had a great health benefits programme, and now without the new job and no hope of another one he would have very limited access to finance to cover his health care. His old boss heard about this and asked Andy to come and see him. When Andy arrived at his office, his old boss looked him in the eye and, saying nothing, he raised his finger to his lips. He then opened his desk drawer, produced Andy's resignation letter and tore it to pieces. As the pieces fell to the floor so did Andy's tears of gratitude and relief.

This story from the headquarters of a tough 'take no prisoners' international firm demonstrates the ability of the State of Connection to bring forward empathy and how humanity prevails. The easy thing for Andy's boss to do was not to connect or empathise with his situation, but he did and the impact of his decision may have saved Andy's life: he recovered fully and is back working at the same firm.

Empathy does not always have to be so dramatic. It is usually more about small gestures. Moments of empathy on a regular basis all add to the emotional bank accounts of those around you.

TOOLS AND TECHNIQUES

I will share three techniques with you that I find wonderful for developing emotional intelligence and empathy and building a State of Connection:

1. Smile and mean it – the easiest technique you will ever learn!
2. Mirroring to understand.
3. Active listening.

1. Smile and mean it

You may often have heard the famous call centre mantra 'smile down the phone'. It can seem like a pointless exercise, as how can the people on the receiving end see it? They cannot, but it is noticed in the intonation of the voice that a smile creates. Smiling is one of the simplest things we can do to get into a State of Connection. Smiling also evokes warm feelings and happiness inside with the release of endorphins and other natural hormones that make us feel optimistic and positive. So a smile has a dual effect: it increases your positive feelings and has a direct and uplifting effect on other people. This then leads to a recurring and consistent *optimistic* attitude.

An important piece of research by Dr Martin Seligman of the University of Pennsylvania on behalf of insurance giant Metropolitan Life revealed that optimistic sales people far outsold pessimistic sales people, and based on this research Metropolitan Life started to look to recruit optimists. As *Fortune Magazine* reported, 'Applicants who were optimists, but failed to meet MET LIFE's other standard test criteria, were hired anyway. This group outsold its pessimistic counterparts by 21% its first year and by 57% the next.' By only hiring optimists Metropolitan Life grew its market share by 50%![9] So not only do you feel great, but it also has tremendous potential to create powerful business success.

You may also have heard the old adage 'it takes forty-four muscles to frown but only twelve to smile' – smiling uses less energy and we feel great about ourselves. However, we can ground this theory in some science. If you remember our friends the mirror neurons, they want to make us smile when someone smiles at us. They also want to make us frown when someone frowns at us. Think about how quickly a riot can spread. Think about how spontaneous laughter can break out in a group of people. Moreover, University of California Professor Paul Ekman conducted experiments to see if the emotions displayed on somebody's face while acting could translate into real chemical emotion in the body.[10] The answer to his study was overwhelmingly yes. If we smile then we feel good and can change a bad mood into a good mood.

However, if we empathise *without* awareness we can subconsciously reflect the mood around us. In a climate of recession the frown becomes the standard face we see in the

9   See www.mindresources.net/marketing/website/profilingtools/ MetLifeCaseStudyMRSSS.pdf.

10 See http://ekman.socialpsychology.org/

media, business, politics and entertainment, thereby further reducing positive market and consumer sentiment. While in a boom the opposite happens, with wild, unchecked, ungrounded optimism leading to bad decisions.

The message is simple: smile and the world smiles with you; cry and the world cries with you. Which do you choose?

Exercise

Smile at your work colleagues and people on the street and really mean it. Send as much positivity as you can, communicate through your smile and eyes. Do this and you will notice several striking benefits:

- You will feel good.
- Others around you will also feel great.
- You will make many deposits into their emotional bank accounts.
- You will start to create a personal and business culture of optimism.
- You will build emotional bridges and find new relationships easier and older ones more dynamic.
- You will start to master the State of Connection.

2. Mirroring to understand

Somatics is the study of using the sensations felt in the physical body to become aware of the effects different emotions have on our physiology. For example, if I feel happy I will smile and you probably will too. It is an internationally recognised method of life and business coaching, where the coachees are led by the coach to become very aware of their posture and body language, and the associated mental and emotional state. The work is underpinned by the studies of Paul Ekman, who proved that changing your body language can change your emotion. This knowledge is applied to good effect with sports people, as it allows them to create the state of winning emotions. Why this is important to us is 'the golden rule' of somatics: everybody physically reacts in the same way to positive or negative mental and emotional states. If we can mirror the body language, expression and posture of another person we will know what emotions they are feeling. With this knowledge as a coach, co-worker, team-mate or superior we can start to uncover the real truth about what people are feeling and unearth the real nature of their issues.

When you start to observe body language you will notice that people who are aligned mentally and emotionally will mirror each other's body language, state, tone and intonation, while those disagreeing or not 'on board' will be marked by their differing physical states. Have you ever noticed that if you speak slowly and deeply and you meet somebody who speaks quickly and with a high pitch, after a brief period of conversation both voices start to harmonise with each other?

The high, fast voice becomes slower and deeper and the deep, slow voice becomes higher and faster. This lets you know there is implicit alignment in your positions. When this does not happen, be aware it may be difficult to find agreement with this person.

Exercise

1. With a friend or colleague find a quiet place to practise this exercise.

2. Assign an 'A' and 'B' tag to each person.

3. Person 'A' needs to think of an emotional situation that occurred recently, it could be attending a wedding, scratching your car, not getting a raise, something emotional. Then 'A', without speaking, must recreate the body language when the event occurred.

4. 'B' must mirror this body language physically for three minutes.

5. 'B' then must tell 'A' how they felt when they mirrored their state.

6. Swap roles and repeat.

What you will find is that you can read the emotional energy of the situation very quickly as you yourself probably use body language in the same manner as your partner. To prove to yourself how good you are at this, turn on your TV with the sound off, and from the posture, expression and body language of the actors or people on screen, try to work out how they feel. Then turn the sound on to see if you were right. You cannot practise this exercise enough, as the more you practise the stronger your empathy skills become and the State of Connection becomes effortless for you. Do this and you or your team will be well on the way to *meaningful* success.

3. Active listening

It sounds simple, right? However, listening is the hardest skill to master, as it requires us to quieten our ego and put aside our judgemental minds. If you are an 'A' Type (achiever), a 'go-getter', fast moving and have been trained, as most people have in the Western world, to provide answers rather than ask questions, then it is no wonder that listening provides such a challenge. As the humorous aphorism states: God gave you two ears and one mouth and they were supposed to be used in that ratio! Our instinct on hearing another's quandary is to make a quick judgement, or rush in to help, or talk about our own agenda or ourselves. To actively listen, try the approach below.

Exercise
1. Using a stopwatch or a clock, pair up with a partner.

2. Let the other person tell you about a situation/issue that happened to them and which they would like help with.

3. Stop the watch or clock as soon as you start to:
   a. Judge what they are saying.
   b. Come up with a solution.
   c. Talk about yourself or your agenda.
   d. Interrupt them.

4. Be honest and you will laugh at how quickly the watch stops.

5. Try this for five minutes and then swap roles with your partner.

SUMMARY

Key attribute: State of Connection = Empathy to build relationships

Memory trigger: Water, Heart

- We have travelled through the inner workings of the mind and know that each one of us has the ability to connect to others.

- Empathy is hard-wired into us and is a gift from our ancestors. It is how we can build cities and form teams and businesses that create real and *meaningful* success.

- Our mirror neurons allow us to read body language, they allow us to get a window into the world of other people and therefore create empathy. The State of Connection is part of what makes us human and allows our lives and businesses to prosper based on emotional intelligence.

- Lest we forget, the first rule of selling, 'people buy from people', reminds us of the importance of connection and empathy in business.

- A large part of our fulfilment and happiness is dictated by the quality of the relationships that we form in business and life.

- Listening, mirroring and smiling are the key components in making the State of Connection a reality.

- To finish – in the words of Stephen Covey – 'seek first to understand, then to be understood' and you can only succeed!

Here is a word cloud of the most common words in this section. The larger the word the more common it is. By looking at these key words it will help you to recall the subject matter and get a mental snapshot of what you have read.

Part 3 –
The State of Certainty

The State of Certainty – creates *CONVICTION*
- Inner knowing and belief
- Trust your instincts, 'gut' feelings
- Dedicated, determined, tenacious
- Memory trigger: your gut, element of earth

The State of Certainty is the most controversial of all the states of success. Many people believe that there is no such thing as certainty. I have found that the same people who believe that nothing is certain are the same people who agonise over decisions, who procrastinate, who lack conviction and who live in fear of making decisions because they are afraid of their outcomes. These people also believe that certainty has to be something that is everlasting. In this way, they place a time constraint on the meaning of certainty.

I believe that certainty does not apply to the outcome but more to the conviction that your course of action or direction is right and therefore certain. With the benefit of hindsight we can see whether our courses of action or decisions were right, but when making a decision we do not have this luxury. At any one time, we only have access to a limited amount of information and using this information we must make our best decision. This decision should *feel* certain as it is the feeling of certainty that expresses the State of Certainty. This certainty allows you to have conviction to commit to a course that will usually lead to the right place. The vacuum created in the absence of having conviction and certainty is the state of failure. The state of failure in my opinion is a state of mental, emotional and spiritual paralysis. It is a state defined by apathy and stagnation. If we are unwilling to do something because of our need to be right, then we fear failure, then we make no mistakes, then we learn nothing and then we do not grow.

I believe that listening to your gut, as a method of making decisions, is one of the fastest ways to create conviction. I am not advocating that we abandon good rational thinking, what I am proposing is that we need to reinstate gut feeling, based on life experience, as an important way of making decisions, and complement it with plans and research.

CERTAINTY AND EARTH

As a memory trigger to help us grasp the concept and remember the qualities of the State of Certainty we can use the element of earth. Throughout history gold has been what people invest in when stocks and currencies become volatile as there is a certainty and surety in a bar of gold. This expresses the value we place on tangible items, material things, things from the earth. A share in a company is not a real item, it is an agreement about the value of something. A piece of gold on the other hand is real. Hence over the ages we have considered that things produced or sourced from the earth, whether they be common like buildings and food, or rare like gold or diamonds, are things of real value. The element of earth is very real and capable of possession in a much more tangible way than fire, air, water or ether. When we speak of certainty we connect the sure and reliable properties of the element of earth to it.

If we look to the world of electrical power, we can see that 'earthing' electricity makes it safe for us to use. Without an earth, an electrical pulse could short equipment in our homes and offices. Lightning rods carry the power of a lightning strike outside of a building so that it is earthed safely into the ground and harmlessly dispersed. We can even use the term for people who are out of control or very disconnected and describe them as ungrounded or unplugged. Thoughts, ideas or feelings that are ungrounded come to nothing. They never achieve a tangible state, but when we bring our thoughts and feelings into a place where they combine with certainty, we make decisions with conviction that provide real results.

THE 'GUT' AND CERTAINTY

Just as the element of earth can be associated with all that is real or solid, for a very long time we have associated our gut feeling or instinct with certainty. Older people in Ireland would talk about 'having a feeling in my waters' when describing a feeling of suspicion about someone. How many times have you heard the phrase 'trust your gut'? When we are worried that something is wrong we often feel uneasiness in our gut, something that indicates something is out of order or not quite right. Our gut is essential in understanding how to become certain and make decisions that lead to conviction.

HOW DO WE MAKE DECISIONS?

There are two main ways to make decisions:

1. Conscious calculation: complex analysis, weighing up the pros and cons.

2. Unconscious calculation: 'thin slicing', gut feeling and intuition.

The first method of complex calculation, or what I call conscious calculation, is based on solving an equation. If we can weigh up all the positives against the negatives in making a decision then we should have an answer that leads to the best outcome. This is the primary method employed by most businesses and people when it comes to decision-making and in my opinion it is deeply flawed if used on its own. If this method of decision-making is so good, then why do we find so many businesses failing? If this decision-making strategy is so good, why do we find that it actually yields lower results than the second approach – gut feeling? The answer I believe lies in the fact that as an intellectual calculation or conscious calculation we only get to use a small proportion of our brains, namely the cerebral cortex or the 'thinking brain'. The second method of calculation – unconscious calculation – is driven by two things, as defined by Gerd Gigerenzer the author of *Gut Feelings*:[11]

1. 'Rules of thumb'.
2. Our brain's evolved capacities.

As our genetic lines developed, certain 'rules of thumb' kept

---

11 Gigerenzer, *Gut Feelings*, p. 18.

our ancestors alive: don't eat bitter fruit, it's poisonous; when the birds fly south, move, as the land will become cold; people who won't look you in the eye are hiding something; the body language of that sabre-toothed tiger says he is well fed and not a threat; and so on. Some of these rules of thumb became encoded in our biology and others appeared as cultural behaviour. Many are locked into our subconscious and are connected not to the cerebral cortex (thinking) but to the limbic system (emotion) and the ancient reptilian (survival) part of our brains and are responsible for our subconscious behaviours and actions.

To see this in action look at a top tennis player such as Rafael Nadal or Roger Federer. When a serve is hit at them, travelling at about 120 kilometres per hour, they have to make instinctive reactions based on gut feeling to return the serve and they use an unconscious calculation. If players were to use conscious calculation, as most businesses do, then they would need to calculate the following variables: wind interference and atmospheric pressure, aerodynamic friction, the number of times the ball had been hit, the surface of the tennis court, the moisture content in the air, on court and on the opponent's racket, velocity, acceleration, spin and many more factors. There is not time to use the complex method to weigh up the right decision, the instinctive subconscious reaction is best. Those who play any kind of sport are forced to make these gut-based decisions on a regular basis. This in turn empowers them to do the same with decisions in business and life.

Unconscious calculation is also called 'thin slicing'. It works on the premise that we can make decisions based on a very small amount, or 'thin slices', of information, which, when submitted into our subconscious, provide us with an answer that is nearly always right. These decisions, based on our experience of fact and feeling, understanding signs, genetic memory and reactions of others, all combine to give a snap decision. Imagine you are playing 'Who wants to be a millionaire?' and for the final question the presenter asks you: 'Which has a larger population, Detroit or Milwaukee?' If you are American you will know a bit about both cities and start the complex calculation of analysing what you know about each city to make your decision. In tests 40% of Americans will get the right answer: Detroit. The same question asked in Germany will see 90% get the answer right and win the million.[12] The reason is that most Germans have heard of Detroit as a car-manufacturing city but few know of Milwaukee, and the rule of thumb they are applying is that if they have heard of one but not the other it must be a bigger city with a bigger population. In many instances we will combine both our conscious and unconscious calculations, thoughts and feelings, to get a good perspective on key decisions.

Similar experiments carried out with stock trading and business decisions all come to the same conclusion: complexity does not equal success. In fact the simpler the strategy the more

12 Gigerenzer, *Gut Feelings*, p. 18.

effective it usually is. 'The extent to which automatic non-conscious processes pervade all aspects of mental and social life, is a difficult truth for people to accept,' according to Yale University psychologist John Bargh.[13] Just think how many good decisions you have made with your gut. Were they right? So ask yourself how often do you trust your gut and allow yourself to 'thin slice' in business, relationships, sport and life? Think of what success you could achieve if you could combine the State of Insight, which gives you clarity, with the State of Certainty, which gives you the conviction and confidence to make the right decisions. It can be very instructive to reflect on decisions we made where we did *not* pay heed to our 'gut feeling'.

GO LEFT

Quite often when successful sports people are asked why they made critical decisions that led to their success, they say 'because it felt right'. In other words, they trusted their gut. It could be that a soccer player passes to a team-mate rather than trying to take on the strike and then the team scores. It could be a rugby team that decides to opt for a scrum rather than a kick at goal that leads to the win.

I have been a national champion in France and the UK in sailing and have represented Ireland many times at European

---

13 In Myers, 'The powers and perils of intuition', p. 23.

and World championships. Based on this experience you could describe me as an expert with very good technique and the ability to make decisions to win races. The reason that I share this with you is to give you some background to a recent race I sailed in. At the start my crew and I, as skipper, had to decide whether we would take the shore side of the racecourse or work our way out to sea. Both routes would eventually take us to the same mark on the course, but we knew one side would be better than the other. We all, using the conscious calculation method, concluded that the right, seaward side of the racecourse would have better wind and more advantageous tides. The left side looked lighter in wind and not as inviting. So we made a clear decision in our minds to go right.

However, all the time my gut was saying the left side would pay better. It was like a little voice that kept repeating 'the left is better, the left is better'. Every time I heard that little voice I would come up with a very rational and well laid out intellectual argument to say why the right was better: making sure that I was talking myself into going right. Eventually the little voice was so persistent I shared it with my crew: 'I *feel* we should go left guys, I don't *know* why, it just feels like it is the best move to make.' They responded with great arguments as to why the right side would be better. Against my own better judgement I agreed with my crew and we sailed to the right. We looked really, really good all the way to within a short distance of the rounding mark, when all of a sudden a new breeze filled in on the left and three boats rounded the mark ahead of us. I laughed as I realised that I had known all along that this would happen and even after twenty years of racing, I still did not trust my gut!

Maybe you can tell similar stories about how you knew in your gut you were right, but you did not listen and take the right course of action. I know that over the years I have sometimes listened to my gut even when it flew contrary to conventional wisdom and my decisions have turned out well. Also I have not trusted my gut and found that what my brain thought was a great move turned out to be the opposite. Another scenario where I see this happen is when I assist companies in selecting personnel from interviews. Often great people are lost when weaker people are hired because they have a very good CV and do a good interview, but when they begin to work it turns out that they are just not suited to the role. Yet in most cases when you talk to those who made the hiring decision they knew in their gut the person was wrong, but all the evidence suggested otherwise.

Maybe the same has happened to you in a relationship – be it romantic, business or social? Have you met someone who appeared on the surface to be great but your gut said 'NO!', and you went ahead only to discover that your gut instinct was right? What all these situations seek to teach us is that we need to trust and listen to our gut as it rarely, if ever, gets it wrong.

We need to be careful, though. Whenever we are relying

on gut feeling we must be in a relaxed state, as fear and anxiety can block the signals or we can sometimes misread our gut feeling if we unknowingly latch on to a yearning or neediness about the item on which we are making a decision. For example, if you always wanted to own a Ferrari, you might try to convince yourself that your gut is telling you to buy one!

Exercise

State of Certainty – yes and no

This first exercise will help you to distinguish between a YES feeling and a NO feeling.

1. Stand up.

2. Close your eyes.

3. Notice your breathing and allow it to settle.

4. Gently shake your arms and legs, becoming aware of your body.

5. Take a deep breath through your nose and feel your belly expand.

6. Take another deep breath, making a whish noise as you exhale through your nose.

7. And take another deep breath, in through your nose, filling your belly and exhaling loudly through your nose.

8. Now let your breath settle.

9. Bring your hands to your belly.

10. Now think of a lie, something you know not to be true.

11. What does it feel like, do you feel queasy, unsure, unstable?

12. Now think of something that is true.

13. Notice how this feels different, surer, more confident, calmer, settled.

14. Remember these feelings, as the first feeling is a NO and the second feeling is a YES.

15. Now open your eyes again.

When I do this exercise (and in my experience of observing others do it) if the answer is false, I feel a shiver move upwards in my belly or I feel butterflies moving upwards and my abdomen tightens. When I feel something that I know to be true, I feel my abdomen relax, my shoulders drop, I feel steady and calm in my belly. You may have very different sensations. All you need to do is recognise the difference between the two feelings and this then sets you up with a YES or NO intuitive feeling. The strength of the YES and NO will also change depending on the importance of the question. 'Should I marry him?' will have a much stronger feeling than 'will I eat beef or salmon?'. Practise this as much as you can. Play with it. Use it on as many decisions as you can and in doing so you will refine this skill so that when you need it in a serious case, it will flow for you; you will create a State of Certainty and therefore have great conviction about your decisions.

DECISIONS BIG AND SMALL

I have discovered that my gut is rarely, if ever, wrong if I take time to listen to the feeling I am getting with regard to a situation or person. This is supported by my work with highly successful teams and individuals. Those who are brave enough to trust their gut instinct are led into a State of Certainty and then have the conviction that leads to success. In fact if you look at some of the most important decisions you have made in your life you will have made them in almost a heartbeat.

Most estate agents will tell you that houses are bought in less than five seconds. That is all it takes for a person to feel 'this is right for me', even though it is the biggest financial commitment most people will make in their lives. It is after this decision that the calculation stage happens, which looks at finance, location, number of rooms and so on. When people find life partners, they often know in an instant that they could spend their lives with this person, perhaps based on unconscious compatible emotional patterns. These decisions are some of the biggest and most important you will ever make and they arise from the gut, they feel right.

The lack of trust placed in people's personal judgement and

gut feeling in the corporate world is stunning. Yet in the entre-preneurial environment this same skill in making decisions and following them through by testing – having conviction – is what creates success. So why should the two worlds be so different? The answer lies in accountability, risk and lack of responsibility. In a corporate environment everyone wants to 'pass the buck', as if a decision turns out to be the wrong one they do not want to take the blame or carry risk. This leads to a culture of reports about reports, about reports, and to a 'blame culture'. The larger the organisation the more prevalent it is. This hyper level of cal-culation and analysis usually sidelines common sense and cer-tainly relegates 'gut feeling' and intuition to the back of the line.

We often see this at play in the political system, where a government hires a major consulting firm to make decisions as an 'insurance policy' so that if the decision turns out to be wrong the consulting firm can be blamed. This reliance on reports enables key politicians and civil servants to 'cover their ass'. The entrepreneur, investor, sole trader, business owner or individual, on the other hand, has to be accountable and trust his or her gut and conscious calculations to create success. This is not easy for risk averse people. However, good companies have the conviction to go with their gut feeling.

I worked in advertising for many years and saw this happen with market research many times. The advertising agency would suggest a certain creative route and, surprise, surprise, the research would usually come back supporting their decision. The research would be needed to show evidence and justification to the client in case the ad bombed. Yet all the time the client's gut could have told him or her the answer because of the mix of his or her experience and empathy. If we had ever asked clients to show us the research that said that they were living in the right house or married to the right partner they would have laughed. And rightly so.

In business and government today there is a farcical situation of report upon report, research about research and plans about plans. All this is bred from a culture of fear that suppresses the amazing and unique contribution that your gut and the State of Certainty can bring. As mentioned before, I am not advocating that we abandon good rational thinking, rather combining it with gut feeling as a way of making decisions.

THE WISDOM OF THE GUT

According to Michael Pollan, author of *In Defense of Food*, 'The human digestive tract has roughly the same number of neurons as the spinal column. We don't know exactly what they are up to, but their existence suggests that much more is going on in the digestion than simply the breakdown of foods into chemicals.'[14] We also know that both the ancient Chinese and

---

14 See http://michaelpollan.com/interviews/michael-pollan-debunks-food-myths/

Greeks believed that our brain was in our head, but that our mind was in our 'gut'. Further to this, science also points to a very strong link between our gut and our brain.[15]

The gut can in fact be described as our little brain. Both the 'little' brain in our digestive system and the 'big' brain in our head consist of neurons (brain cells), roughly 100 billion in our big brain and 100 million in our little brain. This makes our little brain roughly the size of a cat's, and cats as we know are instinctive and clever! Moreover, both the big and little brain have about twenty types of neuron in terms of their different functions.[16]

Anecdotally we know about this connection, as we feel it. Who hasn't felt 'butterflies in their stomach' when under stress or experiencing the excitement of things to come? Similarly many people feel heavy dread in the pit of their stomach when something is wrong. From looking at the scientific evidence, personal experience and observation of successful people, I have concluded that the 'little brain'/'gut' is an incredibly powerful tool to help us create *meaningful* success. These feelings – our intuition – have been instrumental in our evolution over the last 200,000 years.

---

15 See, for example, Dr Heribert Watzke, who founded the Nestlé food science materials department and is a world authority on the intelligence of the digestive system, who can be found on TED.com.

16 *Ibid.*

TURN ON THE SCREEN OF YOUR GUT

So what significance does this have for us today? It is my belief that our 'little brain' in the gut acts like a computer screen for our subconscious. Our 'rules of thumb' and subconscious calculations find it hard to get their message onto the brain's monitor or screen, which is already full of conscious calculations. Instead, the gut becomes the screen and the 'feeling' about what decision to make physically registers in our abdomen. It can act like an override to our conscious calculation mode, kicking in when our gut senses we are making the wrong decision. If we have a NO in our gut we feel tense and unstable, and if we have a YES we feel physically relaxed and easy. This gut feeling is where you get a sense of the right direction to move in, even though you may not have an intellectual reason for doing so. The small screen of the little brain does not do detail. It's a YES or NO answer and this will have been processed by the subconscious and been run against hundreds if not thousands of 'rules of thumb', will have referenced all the books you've read and that the conscious mind has forgotten, and dug deep into forgotten experiences – and all this in a heartbeat.

In my experience, when teaching people to read their gut, I have found that many get a MAYBE rather than a YES or NO. This, I believe, occurs when the subconscious recognises that we are being too hasty with a choice. For example, how many times have you felt you had to make a decision, but felt a strong urge not to? Instead of making the decision there and then you probably slept on it and awoke in the morning with a clear YES or NO. I have often experienced this and 99% of the time I have found that the decision that I made having 'slept on it' was the right one.

Some people call the override function that the gut provides a sixth sense or even a premonition. It seems to kick in most when we are in danger. It is not clear why it happens, but happen it does. It's the feeling that stops people getting on a plane that subsequently crashes. It's the feeling that something dangerous is around the bend when driving that slows you down as you happen upon an accident.

My father used to tell the story of a colleague who was always very practical and never impulsive. One day he suddenly told his colleagues that he had to get home quickly; he didn't know why, he just felt he had to. When he arrived at his house he discovered that it had been hit by lightning and there was a fire in the attic. One of his children, who was at home sick, was asleep in the house! He got the child out of the house, called the fire brigade and saved his house from burning down. My father's colleague still does not know what made him go home, but he is very glad that he listened to that feeling. The power of the human mind is staggering and not yet really understood. My advice therefore is trust your feelings, especially in situations where you feel an overwhelming need to take action.

THE FLIP SIDE

Where we have to be careful with intuition is that sometimes our fears or prejudices can be projected onto the small screen of the gut, leading to the wrong decision. Some ancient fears and 'rules of thumb' have kept us safe, like the fear of spiders and snakes. If you live in Ireland, however, where there are no snakes or spiders that can kill you, this may become a phobia. There are many well-publicised examples of soldiers or police officers making fatal mistakes in times of great fear and pressure. In these instances 'thin slicing' or 'gut feelings' may be dangerous when fuelled by paranoia, negative stereotyping or fear. The death of Jean Charles de Menezes, a Brazilian living in England, demonstrates this. In the aftermath of the London bombings in 2005 the police were on the hunt for those responsible. De Menezes was seen coming out of his apartment building, where a suspected terrorist also lived. Police said they mistook him for a terrorist about to blow up the train and shot him as he boarded. I believe that what happened here was not that the gut feeling was wrong, but that the State of Certainty the police officer felt was driven by the most primal of all instincts, fight or flight, a fear-based response.

The lesson that we can learn from this is that making gut-based decisions that lead us to a State of Certainty, and therefore conviction, must always be checked, especially if we feel fearful. For it may be that the decision we are making is driven by the oldest, reptilian part of the brain whose role is very basic – survival. The fight, flight or freeze instinct is so strong it can override everything, including gut reactions and intuition. Have you ever frozen when making a speech or meeting somebody very powerful? Have you ever felt very frightened of someone and either attacked them physically or verbally, or run away or gone very quiet? If so you have experienced the sometimes debilitating power of your reptilian brain. One way of overcoming this 'fight or flight' response and allowing your State of Certainty to flow based on intuition, is using Benson's Relaxation Response: 'a physical state of deep rest that changes the physical and emotional responses to stress … and the opposite of the fight or flight response'. Herbert Benson, Associate Professor of Medicine, Harvard Medical School, developed the technique when working with people who suffered from panic attacks. It involves breathing deeply through your nose into your belly, which relaxes your body and mind, putting you in an optimal state to tune into your gut and intuition. (Google 'Benson's Relaxation Response' for techniques and further information.)

FLOWING WITH CERTAINTY

We now need to take all that you have read with your conscious mind and let the information sink into your subconscious, giving you access to the State of Certainty with greater ease. This will enable you to have conviction behind your decisions and to go for it. The following exercise is also available in an audio version on www.brendanfoley.net, which will allow you to keep your eyes closed.

Exercise

State of Certainty – make a decision

It is important when making a decision to clear your mind as much as possible from mental clutter or the conscious calculations that are taking place. To do this we must relax the body, which in turn will send a message to the brain to relax. While you may not need to use this method every time, it is a great way to get some direction when you have been procrastinating or are failing to come to a decision via conscious calculation. There is no right or wrong way to complete this process; whatever happens for you is right. Trust yourself and the answer will come.

1. Sit or lie down.

2. Close your eyes.

3. Notice your breathing and allow it to settle.

4. Take a deep breath through your nose and feel your belly expand.

5. Take another deep breath, making a whish noise as you exhale through your nose.

6. And take another deep breath, in through your nose, filling your belly and exhaling loudly through your nose.

7. Now let your breath settle.

8. Tense and relax each part of your body, starting with your feet and working upwards. So tense your toes for three seconds and relax, tense your calf muscles for three seconds and relax, tense the muscles around your knees for three seconds and relax ... continue this process all the way to the crown of your head.

9. Now bring your awareness to your breath. On each breath out say in your mind 'flow', and on each breath in say in your mind 'flow'. Do this for about two minutes.

10. Now ask a question about the decision you have to make and bring your hands to your belly. For example, 'should I take this job?' or 'do I need this product?' or 'should I start a diet?' or 'have I the right people to deliver this project?'

11. Do not look for the answer, let it come, keep asking the question.

12. The answer may come as a word that you hear, 'YES' or 'NO', it may be a word you see on a screen, it may be a positive feeling that means YES or a negative feeling that means NO.

13. If your mind wants to give you more information and background on the decision, let it flow. Take a minute just to be in that space.

14. Now focus on your breath again and notice how relaxed your body is.

15. In your mind say 'flow' as you inhale and 'flow' as you exhale. Do this for another minute.

16. Now take three deep breaths and open your eyes.

I hope that you found your answer, and if not don't worry as it will work its way through your subconscious over the next few days. You might find you get a eureka moment at an unexpected time or when something pertinent to the situation triggers it. I find this method excellent in overcoming procrastination and stagnancy personally and with my coachees. The more you practise it the more you hone the neurons associated with this process. In turn this means that eventually you can make important decisions quickly. Even after years of doing this I still use the process outlined here to help me clarify and make decisions that have major ramifications. In many cases when you go through this more lengthy process it will concur with the initial split-second decision you would have made. So the exercise acts as a confirmation for many.

SUMMARY

Key attribute: State of Certainty = Conviction to make the right decisions

Memory trigger: Earth, 'Gut'

- The State of Certainty is a state that will provide you with the conviction to make the right decisions based on your subconscious calculation ability, which uses your 'rules of thumb' along with 200,000 years of evolutionary ability packed into your little brain and big brain.

- We should not sideline conscious calculation but we do need to use it in unison with the great untapped powers of subconscious calculation.

- We will always, if we allow ourselves to 'tune in' to our gut, have a simple way to make decisions, be they big or small, complex or simple.

- So whether it is YES, NO or MAYBE, trust your gut and start to make decisions that will allow you to create *meaningful* success in your career, business and life.

Here is a word cloud of the most common words in this section. The larger the word the more common it is. By looking at these key words it will help you to recall the subject matter and get a mental snapshot of what you have read.

Part 4 –
The State of Vitality

The State of Vitality – creates ACTION
- Turns ideas and dreams into real results
- Passionate and energetic
- Promotes health and well-being
- Memory trigger: your physical body, element of fire

Quite simply, vitality is the energy for life which creates action. *Meaningful* success requires that action be taken to achieve what you would like in your career, business or life. Vitality has a direct link to your health. When we feel great, we have the energy to succeed and grow, and when our health is compromised then we reduce our ability for action. This part of the book is not about health – there are other books and sources that amply cover the topic – instead, we will look at two main areas that are critical in creating *meaningful* success:

1. Using physical techniques to create vitality.
2. Using mental tools to break the impasse around taking action.

We will primarily focus on the working environment and time spent engaged in the activity of work. On average 66% of our waking hours will be spent, from the age of twenty to sixty-five, working. When you see that, and recognise that over 100,000 hours of your life will be committed to your work or career, you see how important it is to ensure your vitality in this environment. Knowing how to manage your energy will help you to create consistency and longevity, essential ingredients for *meaningful* success.

VITALITY, FIRE AND THE BODY

As a memory trigger we can associate fire and the physical body with the State of Vitality. You know when you meet people who are described as having 'fire in their belly' that they will be somebody passionate and most probably active and vocal. Fire is the element of action. Fire in the combustion chamber of your car's engine moves the pistons that drive it forward. Fire is the force of the volcano that can move mountains and change landscapes. The absence of fire is the absence of action.

Fire is the regenerating force of nature that destroys the old and promotes new life. A beautiful story that illustrates this point occurred in Yosemite National Park, USA, the home of the giant sequoia or redwood tree, the largest living thing on earth. In 1894 the sequoias were protected and part of the management of the woodland included the prevention of natural forest fires. For the next sixty years no new sequoias grew and it was only in the 1950s and 1960s that conservationists realised that the lack of fire was the cause of the problem. They recognised that fires had burned there for thousands of years and many of the sequoias had weathered this, some for over 3,000 years. Looking further, they saw that fire cleared away deadwood and produced fertile ash, and that the heat from the fires opened the sequoias' cones so that new seeds could be dropped into the cleared and fertile ground. Controlled fires are now used to manage the forest, along with natural fires started by lightning.

Fire and action are essential in creating *meaningful* success. Fire burns away deadwood and outdated thinking in our personal lives and businesses. The removal of the old will make way for fertile ground to allow new thinking, new ideas and new methods. Vitality, action and fire are part of a natural cycle of renewal. Look to nature and you see the inevitability of change. We cannot stop change so we need to embrace it and take action.

The colour most associated with fire is red. We see this reflected in some of the most successful brands in the world, brands that are synonymous with passion, action and success: Liverpool Football Club, Vodafone, Coke, Kit-Kat, Ferrari, Manchester United, Swiss Army Knife, Canon, Cork Hurling, Munster Rugby, Target, Band-Aid, Campbell's Soups and so on. When you meet someone wearing red it signifies action. Red is the colour of blood, the liquid that brings power and action to our muscles. So in thinking about getting into the State of Vitality think fire, think red, think action. Our physical body is the greatest vehicle of action, and hence of the State of Vitality. While we may get feelings or thoughts, we must translate these into action if we want to be successful. When our physical structure is restricted we lose our ability to act. Our motion creates action. When we want action we must move our bodies!

THE WHEEL OF VITALITY

To bring this fire to life, I would like you to look at the chart overleaf and score yourself appropriately. It is called the wheel of vitality and it will help you to identify which of the seven essential areas you need to action to maintain vitality.

There are three scoring zones, moving from poor in the centre to great at the outside. Along each line, place an X where you feel you are in that particular area of vitality. So as to make each essential area or topic clear please read the following notes first.

Essential areas

Awareness: Your awareness of the patterns of vitality in your life and the action you take on the back of it. For example, are you best at working in the morning or evening? Do you get sick every holiday? What happens when you do not hydrate enough? When do you need to take multi-vitamins? This scale questions your awareness of the patterns of well-being that you experience and what you do about it.

Relaxation: How much time do you spend taking it easy, which might include reading (non work-related), walking, socialising, meditation and any activity that relaxes rather than stimulates you?

Diet: Do you eat a balanced and healthy diet to suit your age, physique and metabolism? Do you try to eliminate toxins from your diet? Do you source fresh and wholesome foods?

Sleep: Do you have restful sleep? Do you wake up tired (if so, you are not recovering and repairing your body)? Do you under-sleep or over-sleep? Do you struggle to get to sleep? How would you describe the quality of your sleep?

Health: As an overall score how good is your health? Do you have major illnesses? Do you have ongoing illness and disease? Do you feel your immune system is strong or weak?

Exercise: Do you get regular exercise of at least thirty minutes per day? Do you get regular aerobic activity (walking, running, swimming, etc.)? Do you get regular balance, suppleness and strength activity (yoga, pilates, gym work, etc.)? Do you participate in or play a sport?

Balance: Do you feel you have a consistent approach to health, well-being and vitality? Are you a crash dieter or January gym member? Do you have routine and discipline around your health and vitality practice?

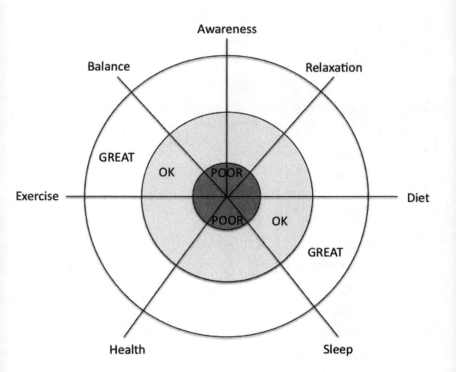

When you have marked the chart with your Xs, draw a line between them all to form a hatched or shaded area. This shape then clearly shows where the work needs to be put in to create vitality and action.

If we look at the fictional chart of Luke below we can draw some very interesting conclusions.

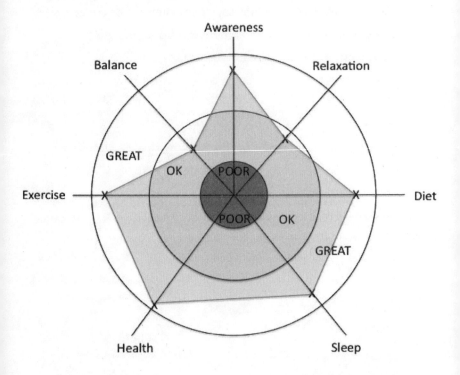

What we can clearly see is that Luke's overall health is great and he takes regular exercise; he seems to have good sleep and diet and strong awareness of his own energy make-up and patterns. The areas that Luke needs to concentrate on are in relation to balance in having a consistent routine and discipline to be consistent in his approach to vitality. It may be that he is sporadic in when and how he exercises, eats and sleeps. If he does not create routine in this area then the other areas of his chart will collapse. We can also deduce that Luke is probably always on the go and does not take the time to relax. This could mean that he will 'burn out' as the mind, body and soul do not get time to rejuvenate and recover from his hectic lifestyle.

The next step for Luke is to take positive action to create the balance that he needs. I would be suggesting that he combine balance and relaxation together. If he starts each day with ten minutes of yoga followed by fifteen minutes of mediation, he will create a ritual and habit. This will inspire him to create similar rituals and habits in other areas of his life when he sees the benefit he gets from the process. The yoga and mediation will prepare him for his day and guarantee him quiet time to rejuvenate.

Exercise

1. Analyse your chart in the same manner.
2. Now outline three actions you need to take to increase your vitality.
3. Now do it!!! (Excuse me, that is my fire coming through!)

You will find that not every part of vitality needs to be addressed. You are usually better off choosing between one and three key areas to work on and then, as these become balanced, move to other areas. I would recommend doing this exercise each quarter or season and noticing the improvements you are making as you take action. In this way you can ensure you are consistent in your approach. Perhaps you could put a reminder on your mobile phone or computer to do this exercise each quarter.

ENVIRONMENTS OF SUCCESS OR HAZARDS?

Given the fact that we will spend on average 100,000 hours in an office or work environment, what can we do to ensure that these spaces, offices and places of work help us to create vitality? To answer this question we must identify unseen hazards to vitality in the working environment, which will mainly include:

- Fluorescent lighting and CFC bulbs, both of which give off strong electromagnetic fields, which can make people feel tired and affect concentration.

- Air conditioning, which dries the moisture from the air, dehydrating you and reducing your focus and concentration.

- Lack of natural light, which can cause SAD (seasonal

affective disorder) and make you feel down and depressed.

- Sitting at a desk all day, which causes bad posture, repetitive strain injury and neck and eye problems, but most importantly, physical inaction stunts mental action.

- High carbohydrate and sugar-based lunches, which spike your energy only to drop it later; this type of diet has also been linked with obesity and diabetes.

Many of these challenges also exist in the retail, manufacturing and 'on-the road' roles. The good news is that very many of these physical factors can be easily and quickly rectified:

- SAD lamps, which mimic the rays of the sun, brighten the mood, and designing spaces with atriums and lots of natural light reduces the need for fluorescent lighting.

- Many new buildings use a natural venting system that allows moisture-rich air from outside to circulate in the building, allowing the structure to breathe. In older offices placing water features in your office or simply keeping a bowl of water in the room will hydrate it. This combined with a daily intake of at least three litres of purified water will help to maintain energy and vitality.

- Moving from your desk every forty minutes is essential to maintain good circulation and to oxygenate the body. This oxygen-rich air then stimulates the brain and helps the State of Insight. Taking ten deep breaths into your belly each hour will also help to keep you sharp and alert.

- Using yoga and Alexander techniques also allow you to stay limber and release tension from your body while working at your desk.

- It is important to choose mainly carbohydrates with a low GI (glycemic index). Low GI foods release energy slowly and consistently, while high GI foods give a quick boost but leave your energy levels lower than before. High GI foods include sugary and processed products. Low GI foods include non-processed cereals, whole grain brown bread, brown rice and brown pasta.

Another way to increase your energy levels in the office is to acknowledge the submodalities as defined by NLP (neuro-linguistic programming). In a working environment they are the physical aspects that affect how we feel, including:

- Visual – level of brightness, light, clutter and colours.
- Auditory – quietness, volume, machines and voices.
- Olfactory – the fragrance of the office.
- Somatic – temperature and textures.

An office that is dark and cluttered, with muted colours, that is too noisy or too quiet, that smells musty and old, that is too cold or too hot, that has rough carpets and scratched furniture, is a sensory nightmare. Your vitality in this environment will be affected, and you will be compromised in your ability to take action. Contrast this with a space that is bright and airy, has quiet parts and buzzing parts, has plenty of plants and natural fragrances from them, is clean, is a perfect temperature, has clean lines and uncluttered spaces. You can see in this environment how your abilities can flow. When I start writing, I have to tidy and clean my office or writing room and desk. This simple act is like a ritual that clears my mind and makes me ready to take action.

In many businesses the sensory environment is not highly valued, with function taking priority over working conditions. Small environmental factors, taken together, have a big effect and investment in this area will yield results and increase the vitality of a workforce. If you start to make some changes in your environment as outlined, you can create some amazing spaces that really facilitate action.

THE PROCRASTINATOR'S DILEMMA

What if you make all the changes suggested in the above exercises, but you still can't take action? Then you are similar to about 30% of the people I encounter in my work. What you suffer from is the procrastinator's dilemma. Procrastinators by definition will delay or postpone action. They will make statements like 'I don't have the right information' or 'I don't have the authority' to themselves and others to avoid doing something. The truth is that a procrastinator lives in fear of taking action, in case it is the wrong thing to do. This is paralysing and stymies all chance of success. To help overcome the inertia of not making decisions we can use physical movement to get out of our 'heads' and into our 'bodies'.

To distinguish between being in your head and being in your body, reflect on this: if you were on a tennis court and the ball was hit in your direction, you would not have time to think about when and how to hit it. You would need to rely on instinct to connect with the ball and send it back past your opponent. Because you are running around the court your body knows what to do; your brain is essentially taking a back seat. You are not consciously feeling any fear about whether or not you will win the point. By contrast, look at a business decision that sees you sitting at your desk pondering whether to take action or not. The physical inaction and stagnation of sitting sends a signal to your brain to do the same: stop, stay still, pause. As we are holistic beings, our minds are not separate from our bodies. Our bodies inform our minds and our minds inform our bodies. When you throw a good dose of emotional fear into the mix there may be a complete impasse in decision-making and action-taking.

To help overcome this deadlock, physically start moving. Go for a walk, jump up and down, get your mind to realise that it must make a decision and take some action. If the task you have to do can be done over the phone, walk and talk. Some of the best sales people in the world walk and talk all day in their office as they realise this movement creates action. The rule is simple:

- Movement = Action
- Stillness = Inaction

Conversely, if you are about to take action that is fuelled by anger or a negative emotion, sitting still will allow you to reflect and come to your senses. I often advise people when using the phone, to sit to make the call if they are feeling angry, as inaction is required in this circumstance to prevent overreaction. If you have a legal call to make, don't walk and talk – this will lead you to be rash and unprofessional; sitting still in this case lets you listen, absorb, process and only then respond.

Before going on stage to give a motivational speech or workshop I will do a series of physical exercises, including swinging my arms, jumping and clapping to get the adrenaline going and to create a State of Vitality and therefore action. Afterwards, I try to create stillness and silence to let the adrenaline subside and allow relaxation to set in. So use your moves, learn what gets you into a place of creating action and into a place of stillness.

ARDA: THE ANSWER TO ACTION
Awareness, Release, Direction, Action

We have looked at creating the right environment and the body movement to encourage action, now we must use a mental process to overcome the impasse in our minds. Taking action as an individual can be challenging enough, but in a group or team it can be even more daunting, as often only one dissenter is enough to stop action taking place. To help us to understand what is happening we can use the ARDA process.

I developed this coaching and facilitation style to assist in tackling personal or business issues. As a framework it can be used to solve or confront challenges or problems. ARDA utilises many of the states you have studied, including Insight, Certainty and Vitality, to create action.

There are four steps to the ARDA process:

- Step 1 **A**wareness – is to become conscious of the issue/problem/blockage to your success.
- Step 2 **R**elease – is to release the blockage.
- Step 3 **D**irection – is to identify the direction/goal that 'feels' successful.

- Step 4   **A**ction – is to see what practical steps you can take now to create success.

ARDA – SOLUTION MATRIX

1. AWARENESS OF ISSUE
- INTUITION / FEELING
- THE '3 WHYS' QUESTIONING
- LISTENING

4. ACTIONS TO TAKE
- PUBLICISE IT
- MEASURE IT
- JUST DO IT!

2. RELEASE ISSUE
- RELEASE FEAR / LIMITING BELIEF
- WHAT WILL YOU GAIN IF YOU DO?
- WHAT WILL IT COST YOU IF YOU DON'T?

3. DIRECTION / GOAL
- BEGIN WITH THE END IN MIND
- YOUR VALUES / PURPOSE
- TIMESCALE

STEP 1: AWARENESS OF THE ISSUE

You cannot solve a problem if you do not know that it exists. If we are exhibiting a behaviour that we are unaware of then we must be informed of it by an outside source. Sometimes we are aware that our behaviour is off but do not investigate further and so we avoid or reject the issue. If we are part of a team, we need to be able to be honest with each other to identify the problem and whether it is shared or just related to an individual. It takes bravery to do this, as facing our issues as a business, or personally, is difficult.

The first step in solving dilemmas is to get as much information on them as we can. We can do this by:

- Using our **intuition** and **feeling** what is wrong (State of Certainty).

- Asking **'the three whys'** to get more information (State of Insight) (i.e. asking 'why' three times to get to the root cause of an issue or to reveal further information – see below).

- **Listening** intently to what is being said and not said (State of Connection).

To increase awareness of an issue within a group of people you might first, watch the body language and interpersonal clues between the group, such as who sits near who, who talks over others, who will not look others in the eyes and so on. Your intuition from this will help you to see and feel what the issue is and where it lies. Based on the intuitive observations you might then ask probing questions, using 'the three whys'. Having asked a person three times why they are doing, saying or acting in a certain manner you start to uncover the truth.

I saw this recently with a management team that had agreed to meet monthly to review their effectiveness, but had not met for four months. They sat opposite each other in their political factions, interrupting each other and refusing eye contact. They were unaware they were doing it, but it was plain to see. Using the 'three whys' method I asked the chief financial officer, 'Why is this team not meeting?'

'We are all very busy and co-ordinating the meetings has been difficult.'

I asked again, 'Why are you so busy, are you busier than when you all agreed to meet?'

'No ... we are as busy now as we were then ...'

'So why are you not meeting then?'

Finally the truth arrived: 'This is not a process that we believe will work because not everyone believes in it.'

I probed further, suspecting that his reference to 'everyone' was in fact to himself.

'Then why have you all agreed to something that you do not believe in?'

'I'm not sure.'

At this stage the head of marketing, who had been listening intently, jumped in and created some real honesty in the room.

'You don't believe in this process because I believe that you and your team are afraid to be accountable and measured, because you fear losing control!'

The cat was out of the bag and the truth was revealed.

After that, all present accepted that in some way they all felt the same – they feared losing control to varying degrees.

We had created *Awareness* of the issue. The next step was to now *Release* the issue.

Exercise

- Ask yourself, 'What issue am I encountering?', and get as much information as you can.

STEP 2: RELEASE THE ISSUE

In every case where action is not taking place that should be, there is always a fear, a belief system or an attachment that is causing the team or individual to resist taking the right action. In our case the team, having recognised the fear of being held accountable, had to let that fear go. To do this requires us to:

- Personally **release any fears** around the issue.
- Identify what we **will** *gain* if we succeed.
- Identify what it **will** *cost* us if we fail.

In the subsequent session with this team, they shared their own personal fears about accountability, which would potentially identify their weaknesses and therefore made them feel uncomfortable and vulnerable. These are valid concerns, and when they were publicly shared the team realised that everyone was in the same boat. Following this breakthrough, the next step was to release this fear around accountability. I asked, 'What will you gain if you create accountability?' The answers said it all:

- 'Being measurable will help us all to perform.'
- 'We can quickly identify areas that need our collective help.'
- 'We will feel more accountable and therefore more open, honest and trusting of each other.'
- 'By knowing that we have to show results and be accountable to each other we will all become more effective.'
- 'We can earn our bonuses by working together to help each other to collectively achieve our goals.'

The next question really pushed them: 'What will it cost you if you do not become accountable?' Their answers were very motivating:

- 'I will leave because I want honesty and openness and I won't work in a team without it.'
- 'Our staff will not be accountable to us because we are not accountable to each other.'
- 'We will fail as a business because our lack of

honesty with each other will mean mistakes will happen again and again and again.'

- 'We will not be able to help each other if nobody admits they have an issue or problem.'

- 'This will not be a good place to work!'

With these insights that they must work together and trust each other, the team could then move to the next step, which is to define the *Direction* they wished to go in.

Exercise

- Again ask yourself about your own issue: what will you get if you overcome the fear and what will it cost you if you don't?

STEP 3: DIRECTION/GOAL

To have a clear direction three things are needed:

1. To begin with the **'end in mind'**.
2. To identify any **values** or **purpose** that lead us in that direction.
3. To put a **timescale** on it.

No journey can begin without a destination, otherwise it is

called 'wandering'. To get a clear direction it is very effective to begin with the 'end in mind' – identify where we would like to be and then work back from this point, identifying key milestones along the route. As a sailor I use the following analogy to help teams understand this: you and your team are put on a yacht in harbour and I throw the lines off. What is the first question you should ask? It is of course: 'Where are we going?' By knowing this you know what resources you will need. For example, a transatlantic crossing will need very different resources to one day's sailing. Likewise your goal or destination will define how much time and effort are required.

Looking at this example, and after much discussion, the team I was working with agreed that the end goal or destination would be to live and breathe the following behaviour:

- We are a team that supports each other, trusts each other and backs each other up.
- We are a team that always shows a united front.
- We are a team that respects each other's abilities and weaknesses.

They went further: Our purpose is to create and provide leadership that will grow the business, support our staff and delight our customers.

With the benefit and confidence created in the team by undertaking this process, they could now outline a road map of steps to allow them to live and breathe their purpose and values. The team went on to agree a series of formal and informal team sessions to build rapport and work in a more aligned manner with each other. They agreed a time frame of six months to reach their destination, with three scheduled meetings of compulsory attendance in the interim period.

Of course such great work will become purely academic if there is no action. Lack of action was the trigger that brought this team to this point and it was possible that they would stumble again unless they took action. The key, and the reason this entire process was taking place, was so that action could occur. A team that can take action is a team that has great vitality and a 'buzz' about it. To ensure action is taken we move to Step 4: *Action*.

STEP 4: ACTION

Having become *Aware* that they had an issue, the team identified and *Released* the fear around trusting each other, and they then outlined the *Direction* that they wished to proceed in. Now they were at the critical point of *Action*. To take real action the team needed to consider these three steps:

1. **Publicise** your action.
2. **Measure** your action.
3. **DO** it.

One of the best ways to create action is to create a sense of jeopardy. When we feel we have something to lose, we are motivated to deliver. A great and positive way to create this sense of jeopardy for the team was to publicise their new route. By sharing their values and purpose with the rest of the business and staff they were 'putting it out there' that this is what they would achieve. To not achieve it would have had the management team branded as failures, something that they did not want to happen. The exact same applies to each of us personally. If you want to make a change, publicise it and your chances of following through increase hugely.

To take this a step further and really make the process transparent the management team measured each other against their agreed values using a score of 0–10 (0 being very poor and 10 being excellent). To further motivate them, their own teams did the same measurement. Allowing this level of accountability and measurement is a sure-fire way to create the necessary impetus for action.

In terms of practical steps there is a requirement for clear dates, times and assignment of responsibilities in the process. To this end, the roles were equally divided, with one team member looking after the adherence to timing and dates, another responsible for the measurement, another responsible for the agenda and follow-up from meetings, another looking after the formal and informal monthly meetings and so on. The role of chairperson for each meeting revolved. For each individual on the team to help them 'just do it', they started each working day asking themselves, 'How can I live these values and purpose today?', and finished it by asking, 'What did I do that was in keeping with the values and the purpose?' In this way teams can ensure that they create *meaningful* success and their levels of vitality and action will overflow.

Exercise

- For yourself, publicise your goal, measure it and go do it.

SUMMARY

Key attribute: State of Vitality = Action to achieve results

Memory trigger: Fire, Physical Body

- The State of Vitality is a state that will provide the energy and impetus to create action.

- The 'fire' in your belly is like the fire that is the creator of change in nature and this can be harnessed in terms of passion for work and life.

- Vitality affects us in two major ways: physically and mentally.

- Physically by using the wheel of vitality we can optimise our well-being and provide the framework for creating action.

- We examined the effect of the environments we work in on our psychology and vitality and saw that improving the physical workplace can build vitality and hence action.

- Using the ARDA (Awareness, Release, Direction, Action) tactics any business or life challenge can be conquered, and most importantly, actioned.

Here is a word cloud of the most common words in this section. The larger the word the more common it is. By looking at these key words it will help you to recall the subject matter and get a mental snapshot of what you have read.

Part 5 – The State of Spirit

The State of Spirit – creates *PURPOSE*
- Identifies purpose
- Creates inspiring leadership
- Defines uniqueness
- Memory trigger: your essence, element of ether

You may be surprised to find that Spirit is one of the **5 States of Success** as it is not a state that is regularly talked about or acknowledged. The State of Spirit is primarily about purpose that inspires others – an individual, team or company – to greatness and is defined by uniqueness and inspiring leadership.

The State of Spirit can be described as the 'X' factor, team spirit and morale: something about a person, a leader, a team or a business that makes them very special or even unique. It takes bravery to be unique, to be special, as society would wish us all to conform to a norm. People, teams and businesses who achieve spectacular success tend to have a very strong sense of their own spirit: an intangible internal drive and guidance system that seems to place them in the right place at the right time, whether that is on the sporting field or trading floor, in the office or home. Being in a State of Spirit requires bravery to stand up for our purpose and to be ourselves. As Marianne Williamson beautifully says:

> Our greatest fear is not that we are inadequate, but that we are powerful beyond measure. It is our light, not our darkness, that frightens us. We ask ourselves, who am I to be brilliant, gorgeous, handsome, talented and fabulous? Who are you to not be? Your playing small does not serve the world. There's nothing enlightened about shrinking so that other people won't feel insecure around you.[17]

Our State of Spirit is like an internal gyroscope that always keeps us in balance and like a compass in that we can gain

---

17   Williamson, *A Return to Love*. See also www.mariannewilliamson. com.

access to a sense of direction or life purpose. It can be intangible and elusive but it is our State of Spirit that comes to the fore when we are at our brightest and best. We are taught from an early age to conform, to 'toe the line', to do as our peers are doing. When we do this, we suffocate our State of Spirit and our unique and special traits, abilities and gifts founder on the rocks of mediocrity. It is important to stand out and be different, to be a leader and to follow what you know in your heart is the right course of action. When you stand out, stand up, it actually defines you as a leader. The greatest pioneers of humanity, science, the arts, sport and life in general tend to be people who have allowed their State of Spirit to flow and most interestingly, rather than being alone and separate, they have succeeded in bringing more people together and creating unity. The ultimate goal of great leadership is to create unity, whether by providing direction or by sharing a vision or purpose in the social, business, personal or sporting arena.

In 1955 when Rosa Parks stood up to American segregation on that bus in Alabama, USA, by refusing to give up her seat to a white person, she showed great courage. Her State of Spirit, purpose and leadership eventually succeeded in creating parity of different races in the eyes of the law. The lone protestor who stood in front of the tanks in Tiananmen Square in China followed his principles and beliefs and was instrumental in China softening its attitude on the right to free speech and opening up connections to the West. Such individual acts of leadership demonstrate spirit and purpose. In Ireland, when SDLP leader John Hume, a democratically elected official, spoke to the IRA in trying to find a way beyond the violence in Northern Ireland, he was ostracised and shunned. Twenty-five years later he was voted the 'Greatest Irish Person' to honour the work he did for civil rights and peace in Northern Ireland. Mohammed Yunus, the founder of the Grameen Bank, a micro credit network that gives tiny unsecured loans to those in poverty so that they can start their own businesses, went against the normal flow of banking and credit, giving it to those who had no access to it. He was awarded the Nobel Peace Prize and the US Presidential Medal of Freedom for his efforts and has changed the lives of tens of thousands by allowing them to start businesses and earn a living. Or look at Irish woman Nicky Deasy who, while trekking in Nepal as part of a career break from accountancy, was so moved by the poverty she saw that she left her job at Ernst & Young to establish Foundation Nepal, a charity dedicated to 'giving a hand up, not a hand out'. To give up steady career prospects at the age of thirty-two to make a real difference to the world in this way demonstrates her uniqueness, leadership and sense of purpose. In her own words, she 'wanted to do something more meaningful with her life'.[18]

Many people have followed their internal compass, which

---

18   See www.foundation-nepal.org.

has directed them to step out of the world of 'me' and into the world of 'us' by asking not what they could do for themselves but what they could do for others. I believe that each of us has that ability to lead. Some in small ways, others in big ways.

I believe the element that connects all people in their greatness, including you, is spirit. The mark of spirit is seen in uniqueness that is as inspiring as it is uplifting. Look at the music of Elvis or The Beatles and how it inspired generations to think differently to their parents and society, to break the mould. In particular look at how unique the music seemed when it first came out. Looking to sport we can see that great performances shine with uniqueness. When we witness somebody like Pelé displaying great footballing skills, or Michael Johnson with his remarkable running success, we are uplifted, as they show us that humans can achieve amazing feats. All of these people have inspired others. The word 'spirit' is the root of inspiration, and inspiration is the lifeblood of *meaningful* success.

SPIRIT AND ETHER

As a mental trigger to help us remember and understand the State of Spirit we can compare it to ether and life force. The mention of ether may bring to mind aesthetic or intellectual conversations about the arts where critics may describe work as ethereal, or ethernets that connect families of computers.

In ancient times the element ether described the invisible animating force of life. In China it was and still is called Qi or Chi, in India it is called Prana and Kundalini. In the West it was called ether or aether, which, it was believed, was a substance upon which light travelled and was the very basis of the fabric of the universe.

The film *Star Wars* may be able to help you with this metaphor! If you are familiar with the trilogy of films by George Lucas you will have often come across the term 'the force', and the phrase 'may the force be with you' has entered the modern lexicon. 'The force' in the *Star Wars* films was the animated power in all life forms. Think of it as team spirit or the *esprit de corp* in your business – it exists, is real, but you cannot touch it. This ether or spirit is the animating force that drives leadership, purpose and uniqueness.

THE SPIRIT OF OCEAN RACERS

The State of Spirit can reveal itself in the most unusual places. I remember being struck by the contrast between myself, as I sat in my nice warm office surrounded by convenience, and the person I had just called by satellite phone, who with his teammates had rounded the most feared place in sailing: Cape Horn, the twisted wind- and wave-beaten tip of South America. As I spoke to Ian Walker, the skipper of the *Green Dragon*, a seventy-foot, carbon-fibre, ocean-racing yacht, I could hear crashes and bangs as the boat slammed into a relentless sea. They were just off the Falkland [Malvinas] Islands and were sailing in strong winds and freezing conditions. They were racing against half a dozen other boats as part of the Volvo Ocean Race, a 36,000-mile gruelling round the world race by sea. The reason for my call was as part of an assignment for the Volvo Ocean Race magazine to interview some of the world's greatest sailors to discover how they cope with fear and stay motivated in such a hostile environment. What is their state of spirit that allows them undertake this great challenge? These men risk life and limb to compete in the most extreme challenge in sport today. So what makes them tick?

Walker, a multi-Olympian competitor and coach, revealed that part of the reason he embraces such challenges, where he potentially risks life and limb, is the death of his former Olympic sailing partner John Merricks, who was tragically killed in a car crash. He states in reference to the incident: 'It pays to know what is important.'[19] This is a man who knows his purpose; to adventure and succeed against the odds. By embracing these great challenges, his life demonstrates great leadership and he inspires us with his achievements. Jerry Kirby, a competitor on the American PUMA boat *Il Mostro*, talks of the crew's number one rule: 'keep it positive!' While

---

19   See Brendan Foley, 'Fear and the game of life', *Life at the Extreme – Official Volvo Ocean Race Magazine*, 2009.

we could call this a cliché, in the cauldron of ocean racing this attitude can mean the difference between life and death, and Kirby demonstrates great leadership and purpose in maintaining positivity in the face of adversity.

Adventurers have always inspired us, from the explorers Robert Falcon Scott, Ernest Shackleton and Thomas Crean, to Sir Edmund Hillary, Clare O'Leary and Pat Falvey. Humans prevailing in inhospitable environs serve to demonstrate the strength of the human spirit to succeed and endure.

What inspiration could you provide today? What adventure could you undertake in your life, business or relationship?

THE VESSEL OF SUCCESS

You, your team, company or organisation is the vessel upon which your success will sail. If I was to ask you now to jump onto a boat and sail around the world, I would be hard pressed to find anyone willing to go. Why? Because you would ask, where are we going? How long will it take us? Who is on the crew? Who will do what? What type of boat is it? Who is the leader? What makes this voyage so special that I should be involved? What resources will I need? Why would I want to do this? All are great questions and very valid. Yet how many of you have asked these questions of yourself, your team and your organisation? Very few I would imagine. It is crucial to be able to ask these questions, of ourselves first and then our teams. Your spirit, your essence, your ether is what makes you unique. Are you recognising your uniqueness and in doing so unleashing your leadership potential?

Leadership is not just the responsibility of the captain or the boss – everyone has a collective responsibility to lead. This does not necessarily mean you need to be the boss, but you do need to have personal responsibility. It is your responsibility to lead an exceptional life, to be part of an exceptional team, and to work in or create an exceptional company or organisation. This type of leadership is often referred to as 'personal leadership'. It differs from hierarchical leadership in that personal leadership happens because it is the 'right thing to do', and this comes from being in a State of Spirit. On a boat, if your crewmate was falling over the side, you would grab him or her. Yet in business how many of your crewmates have you watched falling over the side and done nothing? Maybe it was someone else's responsibility? But was it the right thing to do?

On a boat, if you spotted a leak on board, you would alert the rest of the crew and start to plug the hole straight away. In your life, business or team how many times have you spotted something that you knew you should take action on or sort out yet you didn't? Again maybe it was someone else's responsibility …

These opportunities to embrace our State of Spirit and show leadership are all around us. They can be simple acts or they can be life-changing acts. Take the example of litter in your office. Perhaps you see some paper on the floor, as do five other people, and you all walk past it. Everyone knows the right thing to do is pick it up, but since you did not drop it why should you? Or it is the cleaner's job? Yet if we were in a State of Spirit we would not think twice, we would pick it up and bin it because that's what leaders do. If your crewmate is falling overboard, grab him or her, it is what a good leader would do. If you see a mistake being made by a colleague but it is not your job to help, do it anyway, because it is what a good leader does. Successful sailing teams work brilliantly because everyone collectively leads: if they do not then somebody could lose their life. Most of us don't live in these extreme situations but we can learn from them. When you embrace your leadership abilities, then you bring this way of being to your team and business, which creates *meaningful* success.

Think of the power of a whole team, or business, leading. It would be, and is, an awesome thing to be part of. This does not mean that you will not have challenges or disagreements on the voyage, but together, by being in a State of Spirit, you can create *meaningful* success and achievements.

CAN BUSINESS SERVE A GREATER PURPOSE?

I believe the State of Spirit is the state in which our leadership, purpose and uniqueness combine and unite under the heading of values. Values are what make great companies, according to Jim Collins in his book *Good to Great*. When he researched 'great' companies based on good shareholder value over fifteen years, he noted that all had a clear purpose and leadership that could articulate and communicate it, while those companies who did poorly did not have a clear purpose. Simply having a purpose as a company in my opinion is not enough. If your purpose is just to make profit, then it is uninspiring and certainly not unique. To be really successful in a meaningful way, a higher purpose is required, the kind of purpose that drives The Body Shop, ESPRIT, Apple and others like them.

As CEO Steve Jobs says in relation to the values of Apple: 'We believe that people with passion can change the world for the better.' He goes on to say that values should *never* change; regardless of what the market is doing you should be doing what you believe in.[20] Another example is Google, whose stated mission is to organise the world's information and make it universally accessible. To this they add their ten principles, some of which are: *1. Focus on the end user and all else will follow, 2. It's best to do one thing really well, 3. Fast is better than slow,* and my favourite: *7. You can make money without doing evil.*[21] You might argue that some of the aforementioned

---

20 See www.youtube.com.

21 See www.google.com/corporate.

companies are not the best examples of leadership, higher purpose or uniqueness, but they are founded and driven by some of the key attributes that demonstrate the State of Spirit in the business world.

Anita Roddick founded The Body Shop, a successful retail chain of ethical and environmental cosmetics, whose mission is 'to dedicate our business to the pursuit of social and environmental change'. The chain was so successful it was eventually bought out by the giant L'Oreal brand. I spoke to a lady on one of my workshops who had worked with Roddick in the early days of The Body Shop. She told me, 'we knew what we were about, we did things the ethical way but this did not stop us charging a 300% mark up!' Here we can see a clear demonstration of the State of Spirit but also a business drive to make profit and achieve success. Another ethically run business that is illustrative of the State of Spirit is the highly successful clothing company ESPRIT, which operates over 800 stores and supplies 14,000 retail outlets in over forty countries. Their motto is 'be informed, be involved, make a difference'.

The common factor in all the companies mentioned above is twofold: (1) they all are successful and (2) their core principles were driven by being true to their mission and values which espoused a higher purpose, and this for me describes and demonstrates great leadership.

YOUR MISSION AND VALUES

So how well do you know your company's principles? Are they relevant, well thought out and do they reflect the spirit of those working there (and vice versa)? How well do you know your own personal principles and values? Do you have a sense of your own mission statement? Not one that is all 'corporate speak' but one that actually defines your approach and values in life? If you do not have a mission statement or purpose articulated or a clear set of values outlined, then do not worry, you are in good company. Jack Welch, the former CEO of GE, found that 60% of CEOs attending his seminars had no mission statement and that 80% had no meaningful set of values. Writing down your values and then creating a mission statement from them is very important for yourself and your team or business. By writing them down you activate the part of the brain called the reticular awareness system (RAS). Its role is to isolate the information that is important and relevant to you from all the other distractions that you come across. For example, your RAS is activated when you consciously bring something into your awareness. If you changed car recently you may have noticed that your new type of car is everywhere! Of course cars similar to yours have always been out there, but you did not previously notice them. When you write your mission statement and outline your values you will keep them in your awareness and activate your RAS so that your internal compass can always point you in the right direction and in doing so achieve your goals. In the techniques part of this section you will learn how to outline your values and mission.

HOW CAN YOU SERVE A GREATER PURPOSE?

When we study the science of happiness and fulfilment we see that perhaps the greatest driver is serving a higher or greater purpose or serving others in a meaningful manner. In the commercial world, if a company serves the greater purpose of being an agent of change or making lives better, it results in success. We are no different. Towards the end of their lives most people agree that the greatest things they have done and the legacy they are proudest to leave are the things they did to help others. Nobody cares about how much money they made or what car they drove or what prizes they won. We cannot take anything of monetary value with us when we die; it is then we realise that it is the relationships we had and actions we took to better the lot of others that matter most. So rather than wait until the end of your life why not appreciate those things today? This is why it is so important for you to define your values and mission, for in doing so you will connect to your own greatness and own it.

When you connect to your greatness, to your spirit, you can then inspire others to greatness. As Stephen Covey says, 'find your voice and inspire others to find theirs'.[22] When you start to think, feel and act in a way that is about the greater good and making a difference, you start to see the world in a new way. You start to see that yes, you can make a difference and that it feels good to make that difference, and you are helping to create the future that you would like for yourself and for future generations. This is how we can evolve a worldwide community that has a place for everyone, celebrates uniqueness, and provides and fosters the conditions for universal happiness and fulfilment. This is not a utopian concept, it is a choice. Just reflect on how you felt when somebody empowered you, probably at a time when you were not feeling confident and did not believe in yourself. If we can create teams, businesses and communities that are about empowering others, we create real and *meaningful* success.

When you choose to empower others or to create a team or company vision that does more than just serve your own ends, you create something incredible. These businesses are the sort that attract the best of the best: not only people who want success but also people who care about creating a better world and making a positive difference. Serving a greater purpose is an amazing motivator of people. Research has shown many times that after a certain level of increase in pay people do not deliver more. Also the type of 'boom wrangler' or person attracted to

---

22 See http://www.stephencovey.com/blog/?tag=purpose.

quick success will get bored and move on from your company as soon as things get tough. I have heard it said many times in business that 'we are not curing cancer here, we make and sell "X"'. And therein lies the problem. You can have people in a State of Insight creating great clarity, you can have people in a State of Connection creating empathy, you can have people with a great State of Certainty creating conviction, you can have people with a State of Vitality creating action, but all this becomes ungrounded when it is not anchored by a higher purpose created by the State of Spirit. However, when the company or team has such purpose there is a real reason for these people to stay and to commit to creating remarkable success.

Do you work somewhere that what you do is serving a greater purpose? If not, should you?

Exercise

Your mission and values

This exercise will help you to identify the values that are most important to you and to then build a mission statement for yourself.

It can be used in the exact same manner for a team or business.

1. Write down all the values that you would not be prepared to compromise.

2 Write down all the values that you *aspire* to.

3. Now review your lists and circle three lines from each.

4. Now pick three words from the combined list that you feel are most important to you.

5. Now construct a mission statement using the three values you identified. It must be positive and written in the present tense.

For example:

1. I would not ...
   - I would not steal
   - I would not pollute the environment
   - I would not cheat
   - I would not endanger people

2. I aspire to ...
   - I aspire to be kind
   - I aspire to make a difference in the world
   - I aspire to be truthful
   - I aspire to be successful
   - I aspire to have fun
   - I aspire to be authentic
   - I aspire to let my uniqueness shine

3. Now review your lists and circle three lines from each: the values that you feel are most important to you.

- I would not pollute the environment
- I would not cheat
- I would not endanger people
- I aspire to make a difference in the world
- I aspire to be successful
- I aspire to let my uniqueness shine

4. Now pick three from that list that you feel are most important to you.

   - I would not cheat (convert to positive statement, e.g. 'the truth matters')
   - I aspire to make a difference in the world
   - I aspire to let my uniqueness shine

5. Now construct a mission statement using the three values you identified.

   - Personal

   My uniqueness and truth shine, making a real difference in the world!

   - Business

   Being true to our uniqueness makes us a real company, making a real difference in the world!

   - Sport

   Truth and uniqueness in every performance make a real difference by inspiring others.

Your challenge now is to live your mission. To help you do

this, refer to this statement as often as you can, allowing it to weave its way into your thoughts, feelings and actions.

BE IN THE NOW

You may have been told that time travel is impossible. Nothing could be further from the truth. In fact as you read this you may be time travelling! Our psychological and emotional states are timebound, in other words all our emotions have a link to the past, the present or the future. We are constantly moving backwards and forwards in time, as when we project ourselves into the future or reflect back to the past. This is fine as long as you are spending some time in the now. The now is where your life takes place and the living takes place. It does not happen in the future or the past, it happens now. Some of the most successful and happy people I know operate as much as they can from the now. In the now, you can enjoy life and at the same time take meaningful action.

The chart following illustrates the emotional states associated with the past, present and future. We all want to be in the green zone yet much of our lives is spent in the red zone (past, future). In the green zone (now), we access all that is good and great in life. When we go into the red zones of spending our time in the future or past we inevitably bring up negative emotions that stunt our opportunity to create *meaningful* success.

RED ZONE, GREEN ZONE THINKING

Ekhart Tolle, in his book *The Power of Now*, describes being in the now as 'the power of your presence, your consciousness liberated from thought forms'.[23] Whatever has been your past is not what or who you are now. What you wish for in the future is not who you are now. Who, what you are and what you feel are always experienced in the now. Another way to think about this is to imagine life and success like a good book. If you flick to the last chapter you may get a summation or discover the ending of the story. While this is your destination when you set out to read the book, the real joy is in the reading of each chapter.

I have sailed and raced with people who were only interested

---

23 Tolle, *The Power of Now*.

in the result of the race or in reaching the destination. They did not enjoy the journey and the act of 'being' in the race or on the voyage because the end goal was all that mattered. The same is true in business: if you cannot enjoy the now and all you want is results, then your experience of work will be a hollow, unrewarding existence. We also see in life, business and sport that those who really love doing what they do are not only happy but the results come to them. How many times after a great win will you hear Tiger Woods, Roger Federer, Brian O'Driscoll and so on say, 'I felt really good, I was really enjoying the game' (or match)?

Real living is in the journey not the destination. When we live in the now we allow all of our mental, emotional, spiritual and physical qualities to shine. The leader in the now can deal with what is happening right now in a business, rather than getting stuck in past achievements or failures. He or she can also avoid stressing and worrying about trying to control things that may never happen in the future. You may ask, 'Do we need to plan for the future?' The answer is yes. But once those plans are made, let go of the emotional attachment to them so that they do not cause you worry or anxiety; instead concentrate your efforts in the now and then those plans become realised. The power of being in the now not only allows leadership and purpose to flow through the State of Spirit, but also allows clarity to come through the State of Insight. Being in the now allows you to really listen, which creates empathy and then you flow in a State of Connection. Being present allows you to sense your gut and make great decisions and judgements, bringing you into the State of Certainty. Being in the now means that you listen to your body and create the right environment for the State of Vitality, thereby creating the right action in the now.

Exercise

So how can we be more 'in the now' and release those great emotional states that create real and *meaningful* success? Of all the exercises in this book this is the easiest. Simply breathe! Breathing has to happen in the now, you cannot use breaths from the past or the future, you need air now!

Be in the now!

1. When you notice you are in the red zone (see previous chart) – stressed, anxious, nervous, regretful, guilty, angry – bring your awareness to your breathing and notice that you are in the present moment.

2. Do not try to do anything else, just concentrate on the present moment.

3. Observe the negative emotions wash away and feel fresh, positive and alive.

I recently coached a great guy who was an all rounder, but kept having his success and happiness compromised by anger. His anger came up mostly in meetings so he needed something he could do that would not be disruptive. Here is an adaptation of the exercise that we used. You can substitute 'fear or anger' for any negative emotion, past or future, that you might feel.

Releasing fear or anger

1. Become aware – feel the changes in your emotional state and your physical state.

2. Red zone – say to yourself 'I am in the red zone, I need to get into the green zone.'

3. Belly breathing – slow steady breaths, feel yourself relax, bring your awareness to the now.

4. Green zone – operate from the green zone, listen, ask questions, be present, do not worry about the outcome or bring in past emotional associations.

5. Make a decision – from a place of being present and calm.

I have one last exercise for you courtesy of Ekhart Tolle: if you want to feel total presence and awareness watch your mind and see what is the next thought that comes into your head. Be like a cat watching a mouse hole and waiting to pounce. Try it now.

It took a while, right? Concentration and awareness are key in bringing you into the now.

RIGHT VIEW, RIGHT ACTION, PROFIT

When we want to create the right conditions for leadership and purpose to flow then we must operate from a place that is balanced and fair and invokes a State of Spirit. In a fascinating conversation captured in *The Leader's Way*, Laurens van den Muyzenberg, a leading international business consultant, posed a series of questions to the Dalai Lama, the spiritual leader of Tibet and renowned Buddhist teacher. He challenged the Dalai Lama with a series of questions that many business leaders must face in terms of ethics, morality and leadership of organisations. Questions like 'Is it right to lay people off?', 'Is it good to make profits?'. Maybe surprisingly in both cases the Buddhist answer is yes as long as the same rule is always applied – right view and right action. Van den Muyzenberg found that this concept had incredible business application and did indeed lead to doing the right thing in an ethical manner true to values.[24]

'Right view' means really taking all the factors into account before acting. So if we take the scenario of layoffs, the

---

24 His Holiness the Dalai Lama and van den Muyzenberg, *The Leader's Way*, p. 73.

following questions should be asked: can the company survive with the current overheads? Does overstaffing mean people have less responsibility and therefore happiness? What effect will the layoffs have on the people being made redundant? What effect will the layoffs have on the community? Is there any other option? Only when all the implications on a personal, team and business perspective have been analysed can the 'right action' take place.

Most business success is measured by profit. Is this a mistake? I recently had a conversation with a client in a very big international software company. She was interested to know what was most important to her company out of: 1. Shareholders (profit), 2. Customers or 3. Staff. It is no surprise that most people she canvassed said profit was number one. This is a great question to ask, and you should ask it of your business. As Professor Peter Drucker, the leading authority on business management, stated as far back as 1977:

A business cannot be defined or explained in terms of profit. Asked what a business is the typical businessman is likely to say 'an organisation to make profit'. A typical economist will say the same. The answer is not only false it is irrelevant. The concept of profit maximisation is, in fact, meaningless. Profitability is not the purpose of, but the limiting factor on, business enterprise.[25]

---

25 *Ibid.*

Drucker goes on to say that businesses must have a purpose beyond profit – they must be rooted in society and profit is only a reflection of the validity of business decisions. The Buddhist approach is similar in that it too believes that profit is not bad, just irrelevant. If it comes as the result of great purpose and leadership then so be it. Obviously profit is necessary for a business to survive, but if it is the sole focus then the sense of purpose of the business is lost, and if the business then loses direction, profit will not be achieved.

Exercise

- The next time you have to make a business decision ask yourself, 'Is this about purpose or profit?' Then apply the 'right view, right action' rule.

SUMMARY

Key attribute: State of spirit = Purpose to be a great leader

Memory trigger: Ether, Animating Force of Life

- In the State of Spirit the uniqueness and leadership we all aspire to is driven by purpose and this purpose is the key to *meaningful* success.

- Great companies work with purpose and this not only creates great fulfilment but also success.

- Values act as an internal compass on the sea of life, allowing us to move in the right direction. This direction will inevitably lead us to our own mission and the realisation that in serving others, in serving a higher purpose, we create amazing lives, teams and businesses.

- By creating a mission statement, bringing ourselves into the now and applying the 'right view, right action' rule, we can cultivate a State of Spirit and also activate all the other states of success.

- Your mission is now to live in the State of Spirit and create the abundance, fulfilment and happiness that you desire.

Here is a word cloud of the most common words in this section. The larger the word the more common it is. By looking at these key words it will help you to recall the subject matter and get a mental snapshot of what you have read.

Conclusion

You have successfully navigated the **5 States of Success**. You started your voyage the moment you picked up this book. In doing that you defined yourself as a person who is interested in creating *meaningful* success in your life. The vessel on which that success sails is you, and your crew are the **5 States of Success**: Insight, Connection, Certainty, Vitality and Spirit. The traits and skills that these crewmates bring are Clarity, Empathy, Conviction, Action and Purpose.

Armed with these traits and skills you will have seen how others before you have conquered the seas of life and arrived at the shores of *meaningful* success. These states, stories, insights and research have been a pleasure for me to share. They are aspects that define my existence and they are what I see as key elements that consistently appear when we look below the surface of real success, *meaningful* success.

You may already be using some of these states to great effect and if so well done. What is important now is to identify the states that you access the least or the states that could create the greatest benefit for you. From 0–10, with 10 being as good as it gets, give each one of the states of success a mark of how you feel you are utilising it in your life, team, career or business:

STATE	Score 0–10
The State of Insight – clarity	_____
The State of Connection – empathy	_____
The State of Certainty – conviction	_____
The State of Vitality – action	_____
The State of Spirit – purpose	_____

Now transfer your scores to the **5 States of Success** wheel, placing an 'X' along the appropriate line to reflect your score.

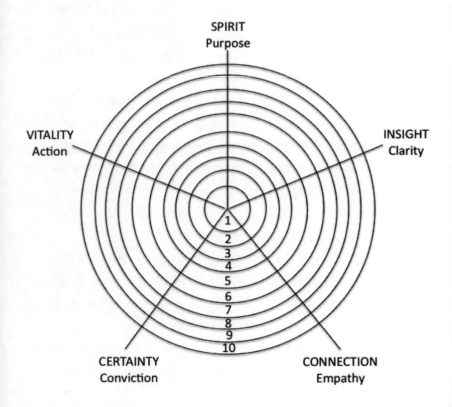

Now join the Xs together and shade in the hatched area between the lines, as has been done in the following example:

STATE	Score 0–10
The State of Insight – clarity	5
The State of Connection – empathy	9
The State of Certainty – conviction	8
The State of Vitality – action	6
The State of Spirit – purpose	10

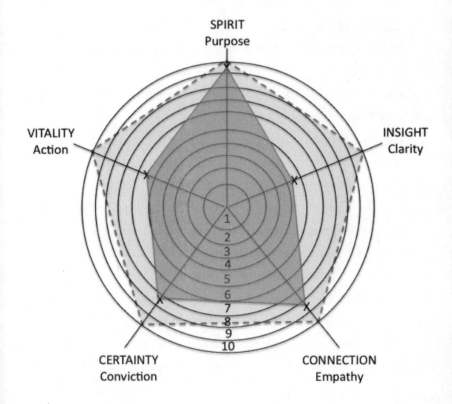

This wheel should quickly provide an overview of which states you access most often and which states you need to bring more into your life. The dashed, lightly shaded area represents that ideal mix which is a balanced maximisation of the five states. In our sample chart the individual, business or team shows strong ability in certainty, connection and spirit, but obviously needs to invest more time, energy and resources in creating vitality and insight. This team/person/company shows strong empathy, conviction and purpose, but struggles to deliver clarity of thinking and message, along with a lack of action and energy.

At this stage you will have recognised that some of these traits are part of your nature and you do not need to try too hard with them, and others must be nurtured as skill sets. When we know and understand this balance between nature and nurture we can structure our life and learning to most effectively target the areas where we can gain the most *meaningful* success. You can download blank charts at www.brendanfoley.net so that you can use this wheel many times or with a team. You can also compare individual wheels in teams and businesses to highlight particular skill sets.

Although the **5 States of Success** represents a set of tools with which you can create *meaningful* success, they are but that – tools. The real and lasting type of *meaningful* success is born of intention. With this intention and trust, *meaningful* success will become as second nature to you as breathing is.

Always remember that you are far greater than you can ever know, far more intelligent than can ever be measured, have unlimited potential and that your brightness and illumination are more powerful than can even be conceived. Carry this in your heart and soul and you will dance with life, adventure with learning, soar with happiness and love with grace.

My wish for you is that you get as much fun, satisfaction and reward as I have from these **5 States of Success** and that you truly achieve *meaningful* success in your career, business and life.

Here is a word cloud of the most common words in this section. The larger the word the more common it is. By looking at these key words it will help you to recall the subject matter and get a mental snapshot of what you have read.

More information, free downloads and tools

To help you to integrate the **5 States of Success** into your life, we have a host of tools and extra information to help you create *meaningful* success in your life.

Online resources: www.brendanfoley.net

- Sign up for email of new content, videos and tips for *meaningful* success. Send an email to meaningfulsuccess@gmail.com with 'tips' in the subject line to subscribe.
- Blog regularly updated with new content and posts on how to create *meaningful* success.
- Video material on creating success.
- Audio downloads for visualisation and meditation.

iphone application: search '5 States of Success' in iTunes or app store for app download

- This is a fantastic little app for your iphone or ipad.
- It will help you to understand and measure the **5 States of Success** within you.
- It will provide you with an action plan to achieve *meaningful* success.
- It's FREE!
- There are plenty of planned upgrades with extra content and resources.

Social media

- www.twitter.com/foleybrendan
- www.facebook.com/brendanfoley.net

Work with Brendan and Seachange Training

- If you are interested in working directly with Brendan Foley and his team to help implement the **5 States of Success** personally, or in your company or organisation, please contact: www.seachangetraining.com.

Book review

There is a catch! In return for all these free services I have a request for you. *Please, please, please* provide an impartial review of this book on www.amazon.com or www.amazon.co.uk. It is really useful to others and greatly helps to spread the word about the book. You can do this at:

- www.amazon.com/gp/customer-reviews/write-a-review.html
- www.amazon.co.uk/gp/customer-reviews/write-a-review.html

Note: You do not need to have purchased your book from Amazon to write a review.

Other titles

Brendan Foley, *The Yin Yang Complex: create success by understanding the world's oldest dynamic forces* (Mercier Press, 2010). Available at all good bookstores and online in paperback and eBook format.

Select Bibliography

Blakeslee, Sandra, 'Cells that read minds', *The New York Times*, 10 January 2006

Buzan, Tony and Barry, *The Mind Map Book: unlock your creativity, boost your memory, change your life* (BBC, 1993)

Collins, Jim, *Good to Great: why some companies make the leap … and others don't* (Random House, 2001)

Covey, Stephen, *The 7 Habits of Highly Effective People* (Simon & Schuster, 2004)

—— *The 8th Habit: from effectiveness to greatness* (Simon & Schuster, 2006)

Dalai Lama, His Holiness the, and van den Muyzenberg, Laurens, *The Leader's Way: business, Buddhism and happiness in an interconnected world* (Nicholas Brealey Publishing, 2008)

Foley, Brendan, *The Yin Yang Complex: create success by understanding the world's oldest dynamic forces* (Mercier Press, 2010)

Gigerenzer, Gerd, *Gut Feelings: short cuts to better decision making* (Penguin, 2007)

Jeffers, Susan, *Feel the Fear and Do It Anyway* (Vermilion, 2007)

Miller, Greg, 'Neuroscience: reflecting on another's mind', *Science* 308 (5724), 13 May 2005

Myers, David G., 'The powers and perils of intuition', *The Scientific American Magazine*, June 2007

Pollan, Michael, *In Defense of Food: an eater's manifesto* (Penguin, 2008)

Rogers, Carl R., 'Reinhold Niebhur's *The Self and the Dramas of History*: A criticism', *Pastoral Psychology* 9, 1958

Seligman, Martin, *Learned Optimism: how to change your mind and your life* (Random House, 1991)

Tolle, Ekhart, *The Power of Now: a guide to spiritual enlightenment* (Kindle edition, New World Library, 2009)

Williamson, Marianne, *A Return to Love: reflections on the principles of a 'course in miracles'* (Thorsons, 1996)

Acknowledgements

I would like to thank my family for their support and patience while I wrote this book and for their unending belief in me and my work, especially my wife, Sarah, who is an inspiration to me.

To my clients and all those who I collaborate with in the personal development, business and sporting arenas, thank you. Your stories and experiences are the raw material that this book has grown from.

Thank you to all the team at Mercier Press for their continuing support. A great deal of thanks also to Simon O'Connor whose work graces the cover.